A
SINGLE
BOARD
FOR
CHURCHES

SINGLE BOARD OR CHURCHES

Lawrence T. Slaght

Organizing for Action

Judson Press ® Valley Forge

A SINGLE BOARD FOR CHURCHES

Copyright © 1979
Judson Press, Valley Forge, PA 19481

Unless otherwise indicated, Bible quotations in this volume are in
accordance with the Holy Bible, King James Version.

Also quoted in this book:
   The Revised Standard Version of the Bible, copyrighted 1946, 1952,
   1971, 1973 © by the Division of Christian Education of the National
   Council of the Churches of Christ in the United States of America,
   and are used by permission.

Library of Congress Cataloging in Publication Data

Slaght, Lawrence T.
   A single board for churches.

   Bibliography: p. 171.
   1. Church management.   I. Title.
BV652.S54   658'.91'25   79-1224
ISBN 0-8170-0838-1

The name JUDSON PRESS is registered as a trademark in the U.S.
Patent Office.

Printed in the U.S.A. ⊕

Contents

Appendixes

Books on Church Administration

Part One:

A Church Finding Its Way

Chapter 1

A New Day for the Church

While the local church is, or ought to be, a stabilizing factor in society, it is not, or certainly should not be, static in its organizational life. This does not mean that the basic message of the church should change with each adjustment in societal patterns, but the delivery systems do need to change. The manner of operation should be adjusted to harmonize with the changing pattern of the cultural environment. The church is a body of people called to be followers of Christ and assigned to be his ambassadors (Matthew 4:19). The New Testament Greek word for this body of ambassador-believers is *ecclesia*, meaning "the called out." The word is used many times in the New Testament and in all but a very few instances is translated into English as "church."

QUESTIONS

At once, of course, questions arise in the minds of those who think seriously about their Christian responsibility. To what are people being called? What does the term "service" mean in the Christian concept? How can a group of people organize themselves for the fulfillment of Christ's instructions? Or, to put it another way, how can form be drawn out of function? Clearly, this is important; for form not drawn from function results in waste, and function not expressed in form produces frustration. Churches are frequently accused of being ineffective and inefficient. Church members are accused of being lacking in devotion and direction. Boards and committees are perpetuated merely because of custom or inertia. New times call for new means; but instead of pruning and paring, there is all too often the addition of other committees and task groups. The end result is organizational chaos. The form becomes one of committee upon committee, of board upon board with function being frustrated and with both pastor and people remaining baffled by their ineffectiveness.

One evidence of the problem occurs when a member is approached by the nominating committee to serve in an official capacity in the church. There is earnest Christian desire on both sides for God's will to be done and for Christ's work to be advanced. But then the definitive questions are asked: "What's involved? What will be the duties? The responsibilities?" At this point, vagueness frequently enters the discussion. The best that the nominator can do is to make reference to that which was done in the past. The best that the candidate can do, then, is to attempt to follow precedent. Frequently "mal-administration" results. One officer invades the domain of another, and damaged egos result; or worse, many essential tasks of the church are not accomplished at all.

Whose fault is this? Is blame to be laid at the feet of the struggling officers? No, they had faulty instruction. Is blame to be laid at the feet of the pastor? Is he or she a poor administrator? Is he or she unequipped with the gifts of ministry? Not necessarily. The basic fault lies with the failure of the church itself to put its house in good administrative order.

THE EARLY CHURCH

The early church was not given a clearly outlined pattern of organization to follow. Jesus nowhere set forth a constitution and bylaws or any such thing. He said, simply, ". . . I will build my church; and the gates of hell shall not prevail against it" (Matthew 16:18). Those were bold and daring words, but how did they work out? Actually, very well. For the movement has outlasted empires, dynasties, sovereignties, customs, and civilizations. The church is a factor of influence in most of the nations of the world.

Why is this? One reason is that God wills the church to be strong, of course. But on the human side the church is strong because it has the capacity to draw its form from its function, its function from its faith, and its faith from its need.

The basic human need is to be reconciled to God, to others, and to self. Jesus declared, "Thou shall love the Lord thy God with all thy heart, and with all thy soul, and with all thy strength, and with all thy mind; and thy neighbour as thyself" (Luke 10:27). The apostle Paul expanded on this command by stating that the followers of Jesus are to be his ambassadors and that God "hath given to us the ministry of reconciliation" (2 Corinthians 5:18). Now, how was this commission worked into the establishment of the church? It was accomplished by a sensible and sensitive response to need.

At first, the disciples came together out of their love and obedience to Jesus, their need for fellowship and mutual support, and their fear of the Jews who opposed them. Then, on Pentecost, they were impelled to give utterance by the Holy Spirit. They baptized because people wished to witness to their newfound faith. They began to share their goods because some of them had need. Then they began to divide the responsibility because chaos was taking command, and this could not be God's way. So some were chosen to serve tables, and some were chosen for the work of prayer and study.

Opportunity came to preach the gospel in other places, and some were selected to go on this errand. On occasion, disagreements arose; and some were chosen to investigate, report, and make recommendations for harmony.

The early church was under way—without pattern, without format. But it grew. It flourished so well—in spite of persecution, the power of Satan, and the general lethargy of men and women to deal straightforwardly with their sins—that in three centuries the Roman emperor himself had capitulated to its claims. What was its secret? Actually, it was no secret at all. The growth was the result of allowing the Spirit of God in Christ to work through the human spirit, notwithstanding ostracism, prejudice, fire, or sword. From faith came function and from function came form.

THE CONTEMPORARY SCENE

Today, people are not different than they were in earlier times. They have physical, mental, social, emotional, and spiritual needs just the same as they did in the days of the disciples. But the circumstances of history and environment have changed. For the founders and framers of an institution to relax after their labors and to congratulate themselves not only upon their achievement but also upon its assured permanence and enduring characteristics is folly. A ship may set its course for a distant port as accurately as possible, but the unpredictability of wind and wave require the constant monitoring of the rudder and the frequent readjustment of course. This is not to say that the cargo, the destination, the crew, or the motive power need be changed, but that course adjustments are needed in order to reach the intended port. In the local church frequent attention must be paid to changing times lest the ultimate goal be missed and lest the ultimate purpose be lost.

For purposes of clarification, it may be well to note some of the forces effecting change in society today. Many could be listed, but seven will suffice: secularization, mobility, diversity, universal suffrage, compulsory education, egalitarianism, and instant communications. From none of these has the church been immune; with all these forces the church must wrestle.

The effect upon the churches of these various forces has been little short of catastrophic. The fact that churches still survive is testimony to the continuing need of men and women for spiritual food and the enduring quality of the gospel to supply such need. However, better delivery methods to supply that need are evident on every hand. The establishment of scores of Bible schools, theological seminaries, lay institutes, Sunday school curricula, and the building of numerous printing presses busily turning out religious literature all witness to this. Moreover, many denominations have endured agonizing reappraisals and readjustment of their organizational structures.[1] Perhaps the least touched in this age of change has been the local church establishment. Here, inertia plus tradition plus lack of direction have combined to make a solid resistance to alteration. To seek, or even accept, change for its own value is, of course, without merit; but to ignore the facts of social life is death. The local church cannot complete the twentieth century and enter into the twenty-first functioning as though it were still in the nineteenth century. Generations ago, Lord Bacon once said, "He that will not apply new remedies must expect new evils." And long before that, Jesus himself said, "No one puts new wine into old wineskins; if he does, the new wine will burst the skins and it will be spilled . . ." (Luke 5:37, RSV). The rise of religious liberty in most denominations, the growth of the lay movement, and the concomitant decline of religious authoritarianism all combine to call for—not a new message in the churches—but a new means for administering that message.

It is not that local churches have been unaware of these adjustments in society but, rather, that they have been too timid in meeting the changes. The usual course of action simply has been to appoint *another* committee. The multiplication of such task forces and their inability to self-destruct when the call for service

[1] See Paul A. Mickey and Robert L. Wilson, *What New Creation?* (Nashville: Abingdon Press, 1977).

has ended has resulted in impossible arrangements. In one church studied, there were 120 different committees. In another, there were 28 separate treasurers. The resulting lack of order and direction in such situations has been experienced by too many pastors and too many church officers. Trying to do their job as effectively as possible, pastor and people become frustrated and confused. No wonder!

Chapter 2

Finding
the Form

If form should follow function, and we believe it ought, then what are the steps in organizing the church? One of two ways may be followed. The first is to dismantle the current structure of offices and reorganize completely. On the other hand, some may feel this to be a too radical departure and prefer to maintain a more traditional organization, but with major adjustments to meet the new demands. Plainly, there are advantages to each approach. The individual congregation must decide the wiser course of action for itself. Perhaps strong and nonprogressive personalities have so entrenched themselves that no real reformation can be achieved without thoroughly disturbing their power base. Or, perhaps, a new congregation is being formed, and there is a willingness to engage in some fresh approach to ministry. To choose something new merely because it is novel is pointless or worse; but to avoid the new only because it is unlike the old and familiar is likewise without merit. The aim should be to seek the form of organization that will best express the biblical imperatives for the individual church.

THE SINGLE-BOARD SYSTEM

When the New Testament is examined for direction in establishing the organization of a local church, it is evident that the early churches had for officers a pastor and a body of elders (a single board). Problems were faced, opportunities were considered, and action was taken by the church under the guidance of this leadership. While it is true that apostolic Christianity was more of a movement than it was a structure, it also is true that authority, responsibility, and systematization existed in a very real fashion. Thus, clearly the one-board arrangement has some biblical precedent, and clearly it levels old obstacles and makes way for a fresh approach to ministry. By no means is it a panacea for all ills, but many have found it an organizational system which is quite useful and adaptable.

Having decided to embark on a new course of action, the first procedure is to discover and delineate what the congregation considers the basic functions of the local church. One church, trying to identify the functions by which it expressed its faith, met in a series of sessions and determined upon the following: to provide the opportunity for worship for its membership and community, to provide the opportunity for Christian growth for all ages through Christian education, to provide a program to win others to Christ, to provide the opportunity for its membership to contribute to social betterment, to provide the opportunity for fellowship among its membership and constituency, to provide for the spiritual and personal counseling of its membership and members of the community at large, to provide facilities in which these several activities might function and to provide for the utilization of its facilities for community service, and, finally, to provide for the administration of religious rites. To supply and support these functions, an organization was developed consisting of eight program committees, or task forces, each with a chairperson. These were: evangelism, Christian education, worship, property, stewardship, personnel, sociability, and missions. Then there were included four general officers for overall administration and coordination: moderator, clerk, treasurer, and financial secretary. These twelve persons, plus the pastor, formed the official council, or board, of the church.

SELECTING A NAME

Both biblical scholars and advertising executives

know that selecting the right name for a person, product, or service is extremely important. Abram became Abraham and Saul became Paul after their new call and commitment. Contests are held to determine the name of a new product. This is done not merely to stimulate interest but also to clarify utility. Some terms have become so popular and universal that they have passed beyond the classification of trade names into common parlance, for example, "cellophane" and "Frigidaire." So it is with the word "deacon." This quickly became the term for church workers and officers in the New Testament church. The Greek word *dìakonos,* meaning "one who renders service to another," was used and became the general term. It is an apt word and well fits ecclesiastical usage. Some churches, in developing the one-board system, have returned to this inclusive New Testament concept and happily so. In such cases, the administrative board of the church is called the "diaconate" and the several members thereof "deacons." Let it be understood, however, that this term is used within a much broader perimeter of responsibility than that formerly assigned to "the board of deacons." The deacons *are* the officers of the church. They function through a number of committees or commissions.

DRAWING FORM FROM FUNCTION

Frequently, there is a tendency for the holder of

an office to conclude that her or his position is the center of activity. This linchpin syndrome can be devastating to the development of a well-rounded ministry of service for all and a sense of stewardship opportunities for all. No task in the church is unimportant; no task is all-important. So where does one start?

The place to begin in the organization of a church is where all Christians start, that is, the experience of being born again or entering into the life of a local church if one is already a believer. This experience relates to the work of the *Evangelism Committee.* This function is mentioned first, not because it is the most important labor for Christ; service is also crucial; but it comes first in the order of events. People should not be members of the church unless they are converted, and no unconverted person ought to try to live outside the church. It is not true to say that everything the church does, or even should be, is evangelistic. The Samaritan didn't try to convert the unfortunate Jew found on the road to Jericho. He bandaged the wounds and arranged for shelter. When evangelism is made the sole end of the church's ministry, untrained Christians always needing childlike treatment result. At the same time, when local ministries neglect the winning of souls, it will not be long before the pews are empty and the teachers have no one to teach.

Once an individual is won to Christ and to the

church, the next step is that of nourishment. The *Worship Committee* has great responsibility in the life of the church. Herein come preaching, music, Bible reading, and prayer. Someone must bear the burden of seeing to it that these activities are conducted in the most effective manner.

Food for the soul comes through worship, and every effort should be made to see that every member is present at every worship service. This is probably the chief feeding place for most Christians, and they dare not neglect this vital act. The author of Hebrews was most emphatic in warning against "forsaking the assembling of ourselves together . . ." (Hebrews 10:25). No doubt he recognized that 100 percent attendance is impossible. Some will be sick. But also some will be negligent; some will be worldly; some will be nursing a grievance. These people all need attention, and it becomes the business of a committee to work with these laggards and attempt to bring them more regularly within the fold. The group of workers who seeks out such people can be called the *Personnel Committee*. Koinonia (a sharing fellowship) was an important characteristic in the life of the early church. It is just as essential in contemporary Christianity.

Then, the church member should be trained in the Christian faith. While it is true that Sunday church schools did not begin until the early part of the nineteenth century and the youth-training organizations did not appear until the latter years of the same period, from the beginning nuture has been integral to the church. Jesus taught his disciples; the early church was careful for the instruction of its catechumens; the Reformation gave increased concern for education; and even the medieval church showed a profound interest in Christian training as evidenced by its multitude of pedagogical art forms. The readiness with which many adults abandon Sunday school for themselves is not a sign of spiritual health and vigor but of immaturity and religious sloth. Who ever knew too much about the Bible? All this training is work for the *Christian Education Committee.*

And where are all these activities to take place? Some of them can be accomplished in the home, and evangelism can be operative anywhere, of course; but from the beginning Christians have found it of consequence to have a common place of assembly. In spite of destructive forces of all kinds, church buildings or remnants thereof can be found dating as far back as the second century. Basic features usually included: an auditorium, a stand for the priest or preacher, and a baptistry. Decorations in the nature of frescoes or sculptures were not rare. All of these presuppose property. Land and space were occupied, and this use involved deeds and rights of possession. Some individual or group was responsible for the property. Thus arose, eventually, the board of trustees. On the one hand, the trustees are the legally accredited group accountable to the state, and on the other hand, they are assigned the task of maintaining the property for the benefit and comfort of the congregation. With a single-board arrangement, the first responsibility will be assumed by the church board or diaconate and the second by its *Property Committee.*

To support the programs of evangelism, education, worship, and fellowship—to supply funds to pay the mortgage, light and heat the church, see that the pastor has an adequate salary, and care for other necessities—is to call for money, time, and effort. The *Stewardship Committee* at this point enters the picture and receives the task. The church will also be stimulated by the *Missions Committee* to look beyond the perimeters of the congregation to other fields of harvest. Then in the logical progression of mission comes the committee charged with providing social leadership for the church, the *Social* or *Hospitality Committee.*

Finally, a number of general officers are needed. These are a clerk to keep the records, a treasurer to dispense funds, a financial secretary to maintain an orderly receipt of such funds, and a moderator to preside at meetings and serve as coordinator of efforts. Walking with all officers, aiding and encouraging them, will be the pastor to whom has been given the oversight of the entire congregation (2 Timothy 4:2; Hebrews 13:17).

Chapter 3

The Single Board

With many people working at one or another task in the functioning of a living church for Christ, it is essential that there be a comprehension of the overall plan of action as well as a coordination of the specific labors. To this end, the church council or single board has been developed. The name may vary—executive committee, advisory board, church council, or what have you—but the purpose should remain. (If this council serves as the single board, it may well be called the diaconate.) It is a central agency for the collection of data regarding the church program and for the review of progress of the church's activities and of church life.

OBJECTIVES

The Bible clearly teaches that "all things be done

decently and in order" (1 Corinthians 14:40). Organization has ever been called for in the administration of God's household. "Moses chose able men out of all Israel, and made them heads over the people . . . the hard causes they brought unto Moses, but every small matter they judged themselves" (Exodus 18:25-26). Jesus appointed the Twelve, and later, the apostles brought the multitude of his followers together and urged the selection of seven deacons for serving tables, which was done (Acts 6:2-6). Thus, over the years God's people have organized themselves for action. To this end, the church council or board exists.

ORGANIZATION

The council or board is the executive committee of the church. If the pattern suggested in the previous chapter is followed, its membership will consist of twelve persons—moderator, clerk, treasurer, financial secretary, and chairpersons of Christian education, evangelism, personnel, sociability, missions, property, stewardship, and worship. These serve as the bridge between the congregation and the various programs of activity and responsibility. It is assumed that each of the program chairpersons (evangelism, personnel, etc.) will, in turn, have a supporting committee and in such a manner many of the membership may be involved in decision making and Christian service. The pastor is a member *ex officio*.

DUTIES

The duties of the individual members of the board or council will be outlined in the discussion of the respective offices in the following chapters. Collectively, the board is to be a clearinghouse for all matters coming to and from the congregation. In order that this responsibility may be fulfilled, it becomes necessary that reports of all board actions be made to the congregation at the regular business meetings or, if need be, at specially called sessions. The board has no prerogative in and of itself; its power is that which has been extended to it by the congregation. Specifically, the board as a whole will advise its constituent members, encourage them in their endeavors, receive and review the reports of their activities, and accept or modify their recommendations. In accordance with these duties, the board will also serve as the pastor's advisory committee, receiving the pastor's reports, accepting or modifying his or her recommendations, and counseling with the pastor for the good of the church. The members of the board shall encourage the pastor and set a good example to the congregation by being regular in attendance at both worship and business sessions of the church, by being faithful in prayer, and by the diligent fulfillment of their particular offices. In the pursuance of its duties, the board may delegate responsibility, as in the assignment of the preparation of the budget to the Stewardship

Committee or the delegation of edifice repair to the Property Committee. Such delegation, however, does not negate the responsibility for review and modification for congregational approval and action. Meeting as a committee of the whole, the board can serve as the membership committee of the church, interviewing each candidate for membership. This 'allows new members to become acquainted with the officers of the church and to receive a brief review of its operating structure. The board also receives for transmittal to the church the report of the nominating committee and approves all committee appointments made by the respective chairpersons.

MEETINGS

The board should meet monthly throughout the year or upon the call of the moderator or pastor. One meeting a year may be designated for a planning session at which time the annual program of activities of the church may be arranged and prepared for congregational review and adoption. Too great stress cannot be placed on this meeting. On this occasion, the board will have the opportunity to review the findings made at the all-church planning conference. The church calendar for the coming year can be finalized with goals set, conflicts adjudicated, and assignments made. Finally, the completed program for the year is readied for presentation to the church for adoption. This latter may seem to be unnecessary, but it is not. All must feel that they have had a part in the production of the program; otherwise they will think the program is none of their business and thus not worthy of their support. The church board is not the church; it is only the church when the church is not in session.

Note: See Appendix A for a brief description of how one church changed to a single-board form of organization. Appendix D contains the Constitution of another church with a single board, in this case termed the Council.

Chapter 4

Coordination of Multiple Boards

Some may feel that such a radical readjustment of the administrative organization of their church is too extensive. For them, the way of reformation is to be preferred. The church probably has a board of deacons. There may be a separate board of deaconesses, or the men and women may serve together on a single board. Then there will be a board of trustees. State laws require a specific body to be legal custodians of property, and there is the need for practical custodianship as well. There will be, usually, a board of Christian education to supervise the church school, youth work, and the like. And, sometimes, there will be a board of missions to stimulate interest in and support for gospel work beyond the confines of the local congregation.

Assuming the existence of the multiple-board

structure, let it not be presumed that each board knows what the others are doing and that all are coordinating their efforts for the most efficient stewardship of the congregation. The concept that the deacons are responsible for the "spiritual" life of the church, the trustees for the "material" things, and the board of education (or even worse, the Sunday school superintendent) solely for the Bible training and activity program is both naive and heretical. Since when was a new edifice erected and furnished without the sacrificial giving of the members? And if such did occur, should it have? Furthermore, when was Jesus aroused to one of his greatest outbursts of indignation? Wasn't it when he could no longer tolerate the misuse of property? The temple had to be cleansed, and it was! If in a church anything is done that is not "spiritual," it ought not to be done, because God has called his children to a spiritual kind of ministry (1 Peter 2:5). If in a church anything is attempted that is not "material," it cannot be done, because human beings live in an earthly environment.

Furthermore, and of intensely practical importance, there must be coordination among the several boards. The pastor, of course, will be an ex officio member of each, but it should not be the pastor's responsibility to be the interpreter, the peacemaker, the adjuster, or the messenger among the boards. If this is the case, the minister might as well do all the work and save time—a course of action too often followed. The officers need to sit down one with another to work out the program for the church. There is only one congregation, and each member is a unit within that assembly. The deacons logically may come with their particular concerns, the trustees with theirs, the educational people with theirs; and the mission board should come, too. All are needed, but they are needed *together*. Since in many churches this meeting of all board members would amount to a group much too large to be effective in discussion and in problem solving, it often has been found that some sort of executive committee with representatives from the various boards and official committees, together with the administrative officers, be formed. Included might be: the chairperson of deacons (and of the deaconesses, if they are separate), the chairperson of the trustees, the chairperson of Christian education (and the Sunday school superintendent, if there is a distinction), the chairperson of missions, the moderator (if this office is distinct from that of the pastor), the church clerk, the financial secretary, the treasurer, and the pastor. Should there be distinct men's and women's organizations, the presidents (or other representatives) might well be included. Sometimes it is helpful to have a youth representative as well. The pastor, of course, would be an active member. This grouping provides a council of delegated and knowledgeable people alert to the various needs of the congregation and prepared to fit those needs together in a compact program for the church. Regardless of the size of the congregation, this group normally should approximate twelve in number. More than this is unwieldly; less fails to provide balance and to touch all bases.

Titles for this administration group vary. One church called theirs "The Board of Control." One can only surmise that at some time in the past, administration in that congregation had become so tangled that, in desperation, the members gave a name and a power to an executive group which the group should not have had. Control is not the function of a single collection of members; such power belongs only to the congregation. A better concept arises from the term "clearinghouse," the place where ideas are sifted, weighed, and prepared for church action. Some churches use the term "advisory board" which seems to express the point quite well. Others simply term the group "the executive committee" which also serves satisfactorily.

By the formation of such a board of review, the various programs and activities of the church can be expected to be examined and balanced much better than if each board functioned as supreme in its own right. Furthermore, difficult problems may receive a more thorough airing than would be possible in the larger assembly of the congregation. Many otherwise competent people find it difficult to express their point of view before a crowd, but they are able to do so in the informality of a small group. Then, there are times, of course, when delicate or confusing or difficult subjects must be addressed. The church often can be saved much time and agony by having these matters thoroughly reviewed and cogent recommendations carefully prepared by the advisory board for congregational action. Such action need not and should not be considered a rubber stamp; but if the official board has done its homework, the alternatives with their various resulting possibilities will have been greatly clarified and the congregational decision more wisely made. Indeed, it could be understood or even written into the constitution that all major matters are to pass through the hands of the executive committee before final action by the church in assembly. The "storming" of a congregational meeting by a determined group, the pressure tactics of a strong-minded individual, or other unsavory but familiar practices are precluded by the presence of the executive board.

In the regular order of administration, each major board of the church may divide itself into working committees based upon the stated mission of the church. One church, for instance, arranged the work of the deacons under two headings: committees for program activity and the committee of the whole. Listed under the former were committees for evangelism, worship, ordinances, and stewardship. Functioning as a committee of the whole, the deacons were the group to review membership applications, visitation of the members, the fostering of Christian fellowship, and the consideration of personal problems within the membership. The trustees were involved in property maintenance. They were not assigned stewardship responsibilities because by its very nature stewardship is concerned with the increase of the flow of funds, while the trustees, by the nature of their office, are tuned to conservation efforts. The board of Christian education was composed of the chairperson and the sub-chairpersons of children, youth, adults, leadership education, and stewardship. Each functioned both independently in the given area of responsibility and in cooperation with the others. The board of missions was composed of two committees: one to work within the congregation in promoting the denominational program and one to work in church extension. Each committee reported to the board, and the board reported to the advisory board which in turn was responsible to the church.

Congregational meetings were held quarterly, and business was transacted expeditiously because items for action had been thoroughly prepared before reaching the floor of the assembly. Concerns brought immediately to the floor of the general meeting were referred to the council for review and action or for report back to the congregational meeting. The presentation of raw data or "unthought-through" ideas was thus handled efficiently and in order. A multiple-board arrangement can be made to work acceptably, but it must articulate its several parts into one coordinating whole.

Chapter 5

The Principles of Administration

What are some principles of administration that should be considered basic in the building or rebuilding of an effective local church organization? How can the church be organized for action? Assuming that the church has an adequate theology and a proper motivation, what factors should be considered fundamental in building the new government? (Of course, it goes without saying that if these elements of an adequate theology and a proper motivation are not present, all else is pointless, but those factors are not within the province of this book. We are concerned here with administration.)

There are seven elements, at least, which need to be present in the construction of a vital church organization. These are: there must be one leader through whom decisions are reached and through whom action flows; there must be the widest possible involvement of the members; there must be the aim of developing existing Christians; there must be the aim to expand the fellowship near and far; there must be a recognition of the stewardship of time, talent, and treasure; there must be a recognition that the congregation is the final authority; and there must be a recognition that order comes through effort.

ONE LEADER

The importance of leadership is emphasized throughout the Bible but nowhere more starkly than in the Book of Judges. "In those days there was no king in Israel: every man did that which was right in his own eyes" (Judges 21:25). These are the closing words of a record which repeatedly reports the sad affairs of a people without a guide. Coordination is essential for action. The human body is composed of many members and driven by many urges. Should one part not be in harmony with the rest, disaster or defeat—large or small—will surely occur. And where is this harmony achieved? It occurs in the nervous system, the centralized portion of which is the brain. It is the head that directs; but the head only sorts, adjusts, and gives direction according to the signals it receives. The head is not the body, but the one without the other is dead.

In the local church, the leader or "head" is the pastor.

Some proclaim that Christ is the head of the church, which is certainly true; and from that they draw the inference that no earthly leader is necessary, which is certainly not true. Even a casual reading of the epistles to Timothy and Titus shows the fallacy in that idea. Timothy was directed by Paul to "remain" at the church in Ephesus and to "charge certain persons" regarding doctrine and conduct. He was to offer prayer for those "in high positions," direct that others should pray "without anger or quarreling" and "that women should adorn themselves modestly." He was to put Paul's instructions "before the brethren," to train himself "in godliness," and to "attend to the public reading of scripture, to preaching, to teaching." He was to "be urgent in season and out of season" convincing, rebuking, and exhorting. He was to administer the enrollment of widows and was to anoint some brethren for special service although he was not to be "hasty" in this. The descriptive term used for this position in the church which the apostle was delineating is the Greek word *episkopos*. It means "overseer" and is translated "bishop" in the English. The term appears six times in the New Testament, sometimes referring to a pastor of pastors and sometimes to a pastor of a congregation. The early church, functioning in its environment, did not draw the distinctions in this regard that were developed later. However, the pattern of single leadership is clear. The pastor, as long as he or she remains in that office, is the leader of the church.

CONGREGATIONAL INVOLVEMENT

The second principle of administration may seem to be contrary to the first, but this is not so. While the body is one, it has "many members" (see 1 Corinthians 12:12). Paul is using here the human body to illustrate his lesson about the spiritual body. The local congregation, whatever its size, is composed of people with widely varying talents and with widely varying spiritual needs. Yet all are called to serve Christ and his creation. Taking one's ease in Zion is not a biblical recommendation for the children of God. The Christians at Rome were urged to present their bodies "as a living sacrifice, holy and acceptable to God. . . ." This was their "spiritual worship" (Romans 12:1, RSV). The great command of Jesus given to his followers was, "Go" (see Matthew 28:19). What a travesty of biblical interpretation it has been to limit this to the disciples before him in Galilee! It is a universal order. We have no choice. How we go, where we go, and when we go—these may be matters for contemplation and investigation; but *that* we go is not. It is our commission. Fortunately, at their best, Christians over the years have thus interpreted these words of Jesus. Unfortunately, Christians have not always been at their best. Sadly, Satan is ever ready to introduce lethargy, confusion, and dereliction. Thus, attention to faithful service is constantly required.

The opportunities for service are almost limitless both in number and in diversity. Within the fold there are property to be erected and maintained, the sick to be visited, the learners to be taught, the needy to be aided, praise to be sung, and prayers to be offered. Without the fold, there are souls to be won, a witness to be made, and a multitude of public tasks in the community. In one small church, a tabulation was made of services being rendered in the city, and it revealed a total of 125 different assignments being exercised. These included responsibilities ranging from membership on the public school board of education to regular visitations at rest homes. In "the uttermost part of the earth," there are mission tasks of evangelism, education, health care, and church administration which have called forth the best from us over the years. "Whatever your hand finds to do, do it . . ." (Ecclesiastes 9:10, RSV).

Involvement not only is an order or a response to need, but it is also an important feature in educational and personal development. To learn through doing is a basic tenet of good pedagogy. Centuries ago the Christian church learned both the value and the limitation of contemplation. To retire from a wicked world might be desirable for the pious but offered little cure for the needy. "Service begins when worship is over" is more than a clever phrase; it is the expression of great truth. The phrase "Sunday religion" rightly speaks of the dangerous error of failing to follow through on the challenge of the gospel. For a body of water to receive constantly and never to release is to form a reservoir of dead water in which no life can survive. Likewise is this true for the human soul.

DEVELOP ALL MEMBERS

The concerned church will be careful to use its best efforts for the Christian development of all its members. It is easy not to do this. Training people in new skills and for new tasks is not an automatic achievement. It is work, often tedious, frustrating, and grueling. Jesus one day met two fishermen working on the Sea of Galilee. He called to them, saying, "Follow me, and I will make you fishers of men" (Matthew 4:19). They did, and he did; but it took three years, and he was the Lord! Faced with the greatest task in the world—its redemption—Jesus called to his side twelve men, and with these twelve disciples the Master spent most of his time. In this, Jesus gave us an imperishable example. It's not how many attend the preaching service that's important; it's what we do with those who do come that is to be valued.

The way of least resistance is to continue the tenure of those persons already in office. No time or effort is spent in the sometimes unsuccessful and frequently laborious work to train new officers. However, the "let-well-enough-alone" theory is only an enticement to stultification. It is an inducement to the growth of proprietary interest on the part of the long term office holder. A certain church treasurer had been in this position over forty years. His enduring qualities were immense. When the church revised its constitution to include the concept of rotation in office and a limited term of two years plus one reelection, the office of treasurer was omitted from this restriction. So it was not surprising that when the congregation voted to increase its missionary contributions—a matter not pleasing to the treasurer—he failed to carry out the commission. It took months of time and agony to remove this person from office and allow the church to have its way. Frankly, he thought he owned the church, and for years the congregation had allowed him to get away with it. What a loss it was: to the man himself for his lack of growth in spiritual vision, for someone else to learn the stewardship of service, and to the mission field for the loss of support which could have been so helpful! One of the greatest mistakes in church administration is to conclude that some of God's children have no talent at all and should be left to sit quietly in the pew doing nothing for Christ. This is an indictment of the Creator, for it implies that a faulty product was made. This course of action is an expression of ignorance or indolence on the part of the church nominating committee, for everyone has talent. According to Jesus' parable, talent varies, but that does not excuse the one with less from using what he or she has. Furthermore, to shut the door of service automatically is to establish an elitism within the church and to deprive many believers of the fruits of stewardship. This is not gospel teaching. This is not gospel practice.

DISCIPLE ALL NATIONS

Jesus said, "Go ye into all the world, and preach the gospel to every creature" (Mark 16:15). There are no footnotes of qualification, no hidden agenda, no exemptions from duty. Evangelism and mission are not optional. These are the "marching orders" of the church. If no "ripple effect" follows the tossing of a stone into the water, one may rightly question whether or not a stone was truly tossed or whether or not water was truly present. Similarly, doubt may be raised of true conversion when no desire to share the faith emerges from within a newly born-again Christian.

The disaster which accompanied the invasion of hyper-Calvinism into the ranks of early nineteenth-century Baptists in America can be charted clearly. By the late eighteenth century, Baptist churches were well and strategically planted throughout the Middle Atlantic area of Delaware, Pennsylvania, and New Jersey. In Delaware, for instance, they were numerous enough so that no one in the entire state had to drive more than twelve miles to attend worship—not too difficult a task when Sunday was the Lord's Day and when a good horse and buggy could cover the distance in a bit more than an hour. But then came the new doctrine which decried Sunday schools, revivals, and missions. The idea that "when God gets ready to save the heathen, he'll do it without your help or mine" took over. Disaster followed and every Baptist church in the state atrophied. All but three have vanished entirely, and these have continued mainly as cemetery associations. The current active churches in Delaware date from the founding of the Second Baptist Church in Wilmington in 1842.

A missionary church grows and a nonmissionary church dies. It is as simple as that. Life begets life. Exercise develops strength—so say the people in physical education. Practice makes perfect—so say the teachers in school. Working the body extends its life—so say the physicians. A similar concept is valid for the spiritual realm as well as for the mental and physical ones. With multitudes of the world's people lying in "darkness," with superstition, ignorance, and carnality in epidemic proportions, how can the possessors of the blessed and liberating gospel withhold their peace? Should they do so, the very stones of the street "would immediately cry out" (Luke 19:40). The message of Jesus is so powerful that old wineskins cannot hold it and old habits cannot contain it. The church must express this dynamic for ferment and growth in witness and in service.

STEWARDSHIP

The stewardship concept is grounded deeply in biblical teaching. One seventh of one's time and one tenth of one's possessions belong to God. In the books of Moses one reads, "Of all that thou shalt give me I will surely give the tenth unto thee" (Genesis 28:22*b*); "All the tithe of the land, whether of the seed of the land, or of the fruit of the tree, is the Lord's; it is holy unto the Lord" (Leviticus 27:30); and "Remember the sabbath day, to keep it holy" (Exodus 20:8).

Some will argue that these are Old Testament texts and that in this age we are under grace and not law. This is true, but so are some other factors. One is that Jesus came not to destroy the law but to fulfill it (Matthew 5:17). Another is that *more* is required under grace than under law. Recall the times when Jesus mentioned a regulation of Moses and then remarked, "But I say unto you . . ." and added a more sweeping pronouncement. Think, too, of Paul's clarion call to service, "I beseech you therefore, brethren, by the mercies of God, that ye present your bodies a living sacrifice, holy, acceptable unto God, which is your reasonable service" (Romans 12:1). Is the Christian to give less out of love than the Jew was to give on the basis of law? Of course not.

When the nominating committee approaches a church member with a request for service, it should not be done with an apologetic attitude. It should not be done in the context of "this won't take much time." Such apologies cheapen the church, violate the Scriptures, and demean Christ. "Give of your best to the Master" is not just the verse from a fine hymn; it is an authoritative pronouncement. Christians, and the churches to which they belong, are headed straight for trouble when anything less than serious sacrifice is suggested.

This does not mean, however, that a few should do all the work. It means, rather, that careful planning should be done in developing an organization that will allow a sharing of obligations. Unless this is done, some willing workers will be overextended and some lazy folk will not do their part. The latter will lose the blessing, and the former may say, "Never again." Both are sad results and neither fulfills Paul's injunction for "reasonable service." One way of establishing equalization of time demands is to make a survey of various tasks noting a normal commitment; e.g., a member of the choir puts in so much time in general rehearsal, private rehearsal, and public presentation. A Sunday school teacher puts in so much time in lesson preparation, in pupil visitation, and in class instruction. A series of informal and nontechnical studies such as these can be very helpful in stimulating the lethargic and giving direction to the overly committed. How much time does it take the financial secretary to count, record, and deposit the gifts of the congregation? Can a deacon fulfill the time obligation by serving Communion once a month and by attending a meeting of the board?

As for the stewardship of treasure, the question is not, "What is *my* share?" Rather, it is, "What is *God's* share?" A prosperous businessman was a faithful member of the church and a regular giver. He gave one dollar every week! For some this would have been sacrificial; for him it was disgraceful (and that word here should be read in its theological meaning as well as its sociological one). When faced with the issue, the defense given was, "What's the problem? The church's bills are paid every month. We have no debt." "The problem lies within yourself" was the answer. "You need to give more than God needs the money. Think of what the church could do if it had the funds." Since both husband and wife truly were good Christians, they began to study their stewardship habits in relationship to the Scriptures. Needless to say, they found their habits out of harmony with the Bible and they began at once to rectify matters. Three results followed. The church closed its next year's books with a balance in the bank of eight thousand dollars. New ventures for Christ were sought and developed so that the added income could be put to work. And joy that had not been known before entered the couple's lives.

CONGREGATIONAL AUTHORITY

In the decision-making process, there must be a

point and a place where judgment is reached. In churches with an episcopal form of government, this jurisdiction lies with the bishop. In churches with a representative form of government, this lies with the synod or general assembly. But with churches following the congregational arrangement, the local church is its own master. To be sure, the lines are not as distinct as the words imply. Even in an authoritarian arrangement, the individual believers and the individual assembly of believers have more than a little influence. And in a theoretically democratic society, equality may vary. Paul Harrison demonstrated this amply in his book *Authority and Power in the Free Church Tradition*.[1]

Nevertheless, there is a place for final decision in the congregational establishment, and that place is the local church itself. This sovereignty lies not with the pastor, the board of deacons, or other official body, or with the regional or national organization. It lies not with some individual within the group, but it lies with the local church in assembly. Herein are problems aplenty, but let no congregationalist think that episcopacy or presbytery is without problems. Each form of ecclesiastical order is subject to its own deficiency. Perfection is heavenly, not earthly.

In the fifteenth chapter of the Acts of the Apostles is

[1] Paul Harrison, *Authority and Power in the Free Church Tradition* (Princeton: Princeton University Press, 1959).

found one of the first and one of the finest references to the work of a body of believers engaged in problem solving. The situation was that the gospel was being preached at Antioch and some Gentile people were believing and being saved. This disturbed the Judaizers who held that circumcision "after the manner of Moses" was necessary for salvation (Acts 15:1). This was a serious matter. Did one have to become a Jew first in order to become a Christian? If so, then much Christian doctrine would have to be changed, and the future of the whole work of Christ would move in another direction. It is not unreasonable to suppose that by so identifying the gospel with Judaism, the whole movement would have gone down with the collapse of Jerusalem under the Romans. This disaster was avoided by the early church taking a firm stand for self-identity. Note the steps: (1) the problem stated—15:1; (2) representatives appointed by the assembly in Antioch to go to Jerusalem—15:2; (3) the joyful reception by the church there—15:4; (4) the presentation before the multitude or assembly—15:6, 12; (5) the debate—15:5, 7-12; (6) the summation and recommendation—15:13-21; and (7) the decision and response—15:22-29. A key principle of procedure is stated in verse 25: "It seemed good unto us, being assembled with one accord. . . ." They were assembled together, and they were in harmony one with another. In consequence, they faced squarely a most troublesome situation and reached a solution sound enough to endure for the ages. This was congregational action at its best.

The local church faced its problem openly. An appeal was made to other Christians sincerely. An honest discussion was held, and a clear-cut decision was reached. When this decision was shared with the inquiring church, it was received with rejoicing (Acts 15:31). The local church must stand on its own base, but it does not stand isolated or lonely. The body of Christ is greater than any single group of believers or any combination thereof. Church cooperation, both within the denomination and without, is important not only for the contribution which the local church can render through such contacts, but also for the contributions which can be received. A congregation should not congratulate itself but, rather, should take alarm if it begins to believe that it alone has all the truth. Congregational authority, while regnant, is not omniscient; and while it is authoritative, it is not authoritarian. It must have the position of power, but it dare not maintain the posture of demanding blind obedience. Christians need to remind themselves that they "have this treasure in earthen vessels"; for if they do not, the excellency of the power of God may not be manifest (2 Corinthians 4:7).

STRIVING FOR ORDER

Unfortunately, not all church assemblies have

been as united in spirit and as determined in character as the church in Jerusalem, nor have all churches been as inquiring in spirit as the congregation at Antioch. God made cosmos, not chaos; but men and women have not been as careful in their own creations. Adam and Eve discovered even paradise was not to their complete satisfaction and found ways to disturb it. Their sons and daughters have been equally successful in achieving disharmony. Satan, that great deceiver, of course, has been at the root of ruin; but to state this has not been to cure the condition. Order is achieved by sacrifice and struggle. This has been the story of the Bible. This was the story of the altars in the Old Testament, the cross of Calvary in the Gospels, or the account of the overcomers in the book of Revelation.

No body of Christians has ever been perfect, either within its individual constituents or among them. Wherever people have been found, sin has been found, also. Jesus saw that his disciples could be far from perfect. Peter could curse and lie; Thomas could doubt; James and John could be overly ambitious; Judas could betray his Master; and they all could abandon him in the time of trial. Yet this same group could form the first church and carry its message to the far reaches of the Roman world.

This great achievement was accomplished not because of weakness but in spite of it. Body, mind, and spirit were devoted to the task. Their bodies suffered in prisons from Caesarea to Rome, and some were committed unto death. Their minds were set on a course of study to show themselves "approved unto God." Their spirits were open to His Spirit for conversion, for confirmation in trial, and for instruction in righteousness and in mission.

Thus, it should come as no surprise that establishing an effective organization for service by the local church demands the highest effort by all involved. Experiences of reversals will occur because of human limitation, both natural and designed (1 Corinthians 1:11-13); because of Satanic influence (1 Peter 5:8); and, sometimes, because it is God's will that obedience be learned through suffering (Hebrews 5:8). The items of importance, as the context of these references show, are these: (1) *Be faithful unto Christ.* They who try to enter the kingdom any other way are like thieves and robbers. Only Jesus is the door (John 10:1-7). (2) *Resist evil.* Casting one's care upon God does not free the believer from conflict; rather, it allows the heavenly power to flow more freely because of the sobriety and readiness present. The faithful are not redeemed from conflict; they are redeemed for conflict. In this regard, it would be good to review John's teaching in the book of Revelation; all inhabitants of the earth die. Some die for Christ (Revelation 7:14; 18:24), and some die for themselves (13:8; 18:3, 24). The difference lies in allegiance, a true record of which is found either in the book of life or the books of works (20:12). Peter wrote words of great wisdom when he remarked, "Beloved, think it not strange concerning the fiery trial which is to try you, as though something happened unto you: But rejoice, inasmuch as ye are partakers of Christ's sufferings. . . ." (1 Peter 4:12-13). (3) *Grow up.* Christians should mature. As it is written, "Strong meat belongeth to them that are of full age, even those who by reason of use have their senses exercised to discern both good and evil" (Hebrews 5:14). Accept the sovereignty of God! Remember the trenchant remark of Charles H. Spurgeon: "As sure as ever God puts His children in the furnace, He will be in the furnace with them." And where God is, there is victory.

A group of believers setting out to form a new church, or to reform an established one, must observe these rules: be faithful unto Christ, resist evil, and make every effort to mature. It will not be easy. Sadly, many assume the naive position that once one becomes a Christian, all problems are solved; and once one becomes a member of the church, all behavior patterns automatically become controlled by the Holy Spirit. These items just are not true. The apostle Paul's frequent reference to the Christian life in martial terms was no accident. It came out of ripe experience. Vital congregations do not descend out of heaven but are gathered on earth by laborious process. Sometimes the realities of this come as a surprise and as a shock, and earnest Christians falter in the task of building a gospel church. Then, as an insult to the Christ who served them and in disobedience to the Savior who commissioned them, they abandon the work. This should not be. This need not be, but what must be is a recognition that the assignment is a serious and severe one and that steadiness and strength are essential for its accomplishment.

Part Two:

Functional Committees

Chapter 6

The Evangelism Committee

A congregation of Christian believers does not just happen. Something must be done to draw them to Christ and to one another. But what? And how? Who is to do the drawing? And which others are to be added to the initial group? In the answering of these questions, there emerges the description of the work of the Evangelism Committee.

OBJECTIVES

Evangelism may be said to be a threefold process. The first part is that of leading an individual to accept Jesus Christ as personal Savior and Lord of all life. Here, the task is so to witness for Christ that the Holy Spirit may have an open opportunity to do the work of regeneration. No one should join the church who cannot offer evidence by word and deed that this change has occurred. The application of water on the body— through either immersion or sprinkling—will not accomplish this. The promise of godly parents or friends will not suffice. The careful recitation of the creed will not satisfy, nor will the study and discussion of the same give the answer. Jesus said, "Ye must be born again" (John 3:7*b*). This is not optional, but foundational. This is not to say that everyone must have an experience like Saul on the road to Damascus. After all, how many Sauls of Tarsus were there? Conversion is an individual matter, experienced in a unique way and expressed in a singular fashion. New Christians are not produced *en masse* or by assembly-line methods but by the direct and specific encounter of an individual with Christ.

This second step in the process of evangelism is the introduction and inclusion of the born again into the life of the local church. Many evangelists, both lay and professional, in times past have neglected or ignored this important step. They have, thereby, both demeaned their calling and harmed the work. The evangelist cannot be said to have completed the assignment until the convert has been integrated into the life of the church.

The third step in evangelism is the leading of the newly converted, or the newly committed to the church, to engage in the winning of others. The attrition rate of new members in the normal congregation is much too high. Some say it averages 50 percent. This is a sad loss from every standpoint, but it can be lessened by putting the newcomer promptly into the business of exercising his or her soul through witnessing. Nothing cleanses the spirit and clarifies the mind so effectively as doing the work of an evangelist. It is true that some are better fitted for the task than others. It is true that some will find it possible to be more active than others. But none in the church should consider oneself exempt from this calling. A witnessing church will be a thriving church—anytime, anywhere.

"And the lord said unto the servant, Go out into the highways and hedges, and compel them to come in, that my house may be filled" (Luke 14:23).

ORGANIZATION

The organization for evangelistic effort in the local church need not be elaborate. Responsibility for the formulation and execution of the program of witness, recruitment, and integration may be vested in a committee composed of a chairperson and as few as two other members. Some churches may decide to increase the size of the group, but for administrative purposes the number should be fairly limited. The chairperson should, of course, be a member of the executive board of the church and should be recognized by one and all as the individual giving point and promise to the work of evangelism. This effort should not and must not be left to the pastor. Jesus trained his disciples; his disciples trained others; and everyone went to work. Certainly the fields "are white already to harvest" (see John 4:35). Certainly "the labourers are few" (see Matthew 9:37). Jesus said, "The night cometh, when no man can work" (John 9:4*b*).

DUTIES

What specific duties are to be performed by the Evangelism Committee in fulfillment of its assigned service? What might be considered the form of its function as it arranges the work of witness?

Consider, in this regard, two categories of people: those who come through the doors of the church and those who don't. A nonmember who enters the church for any reason—to attend Sunday school or worship service, to counsel with the pastor, to listen to a concert—offers some potential as a prospect. The Evangelism Committee, therefore, will be diligent to see that all such visitors are welcomed (if it be a public activity); and their names, addresses, phone numbers, and religious affiliation are to be obtained in as unobtrusive but effective a fashion as possible. The introduction to the pastor will be considered highly important. Similarly, should the pastor or someone else within the church be the contact person, the identifying data should be passed along to the evangelism chairperson. Many congregations have greeters in the vestibule of the church for all major worship services. These people can be very helpful in serving as a bridge between the world and the sanctuary, between the newcomer and the established members, between the non-Christian and the Christian. The committee will see that greeters are present and active. A smile and a handshake are good, but more is involved. Who are these people who drop by, and how can the church minister to them?

The responsibility of the Evangelism Committee is to see that prompt follow-up calls are made on all visitors. A letter is good, even a mimeographed or printed one, but a personal visit is better. Again, this is not the assignment of the pastor primarily, although he or she will surely do his or her share. The committee may choose to set aside one day (or evening) each week (or each month) when teams of two persons each go out on visitation. Such occasions are splendid opportunities for the pastor and others who are skilled in witnessing to train those with less experience. A church filled with regular witnesses can be assured of being filled with regular worshipers.

To catch the attention of those in the area who do not enter the church edifice under any guise, the committee may wish to sponsor house-to-house surveys, newspaper advertising, radio and television announcements, the broadcast of regular or special services, and news release items—all this being done in the effort to spread the word around and in the expectation of winning some. The distribution of tracts or other Gospel literature may also be fostered. At least one special evangelistic effort should be undertaken each year. And the pastor should be encouraged to keep the sermons warm with gospel fervor and to extend at frequent intervals a public invitation to accept Christ and/or unite with the church. While it may be true that an invitation every Sunday in a static congregation may produce a spirit of nonexpectation, to give an invitation seldom or never is unforgivable.

Of course, the Evangelism Committee will work closely with the Christian Education Committee in the fostering of Sunday school growth and in the bringing of enrollees to a decision for Christ when they reach the age of accountability. Building Sunday school attendance is as much the task of the Evangelism Committee as is the building of worship attendance. Both study and worship are functions of the church, and both experiences are needed by the respective members. Recruitment is the watchword for the Evangelism Committee, and this covers both phases of church life. Thus, the Evangelism Committee will also maintain contact with the Worship Committee so that proper soul-winning emphasis and strategies may be present in the services of worship.

To assure completeness and coordination, a prospect

list of friends, visitors, and possible church members is to be maintained by the Evangelism Committee. Various schemes are useful, but whatever is done, the file should be complete with name, address, phone number, religious background, current affiliation (if any), record of previous visits (if there have been any), and the results obtained or the judgment of the caller. This data should be so arranged and so placed as to be readily available to both pastor and evangelism chairperson.

Materials for the use of the committee are obtainable from denominational publishing houses, Bible bookstores, and a wide variety of independent publishers. There is a vast array of printed supplies, but these do no good stacked in a warehouse or standing in a rack. They require distribution. More importantly, the average congregation needs to be awakened to the fact that the majority of visitors who attend church do so because someone has *invited* them! The popularity of the preacher, the reputation of the church, the beauty of the music will never be as attractive as the warm words of a friend, "I'd be pleased to take you to my church some Sunday. I think you would like it." Promoting such a spirit throughout the congregation is the business of the Evangelism Committee.

Chapter 7

The Worship Committee

It has been observed that no race of people has ever been found which was so primitive, or so sophisticated, that it had no place for worship in its culture. The object of worship, the means, method, and motive might vary. Involved could be a bright feather, a mountain, an animal, or matter in outer space. Involved could be a glorification of human instincts or a spiritual concept of the highest order. But always there is a reverence toward that which is beyond self and a ritual practiced which gives expression to that reverence. Worship at its best—certainly Christian worship—has nurture implied, also. The late President Calvin Coolidge once said, "It is only when men begin to worship that they begin to grow." If baptism connotes birth—and it does—and if the Lord's Supper suggests sustenance—

and it does—surely the importance of frequent and regular participation in worship experiences for the development of believers should be practiced. The church will offer every possible opportunity to fulfill this need for worship.

OBJECTIVES

The prophet Isaiah said, speaking for God, "Incline your ear, and come unto me: hear, and your soul shall live" (Isaiah 55:3a). The objective of Christian worship is to bring into communion those who are searching and the God who is supplying, to the end that the believers are established in holiness and the saints are strengthened for witness. Augustine once said, "Thou, O God, hath made us for thyself, and we are restless until we find our rest in Thee." Jesus regularly attended the synagogue service and was frequently in the temple. His disciples continued this custom and added to it Sunday worship and frequent meeting for prayer. A Christian, or a group of Christians, may abandon much or alter much as faith is developed, but worship is abandoned only at the point and price of spiritual starvation. In atheistic, communist countries, death often has been the price of worship as it was in imperial Rome; but faithful Christians have not wavered.

The Worship Committee of the local church has as its objective the providing of the means to and the

stimulation of motivation for the worship of God in
Jesus Christ through the Holy Spirit. The Worship
Committee is not to be just a decorating committee or
just an ushering committee or just a music committee
or just an ordinance committee. All of these activities
may be included, but more is involved. If the
congregation, for instance, meets at 11 o'clock on
Sunday morning for public worship and at 8 o'clock on
Thursday evening for prayer meeting, everything that
transpires at those times is of concern to the Worship
Committee.

ORGANIZATION

The Worship Committee may want to function
on a two-tier basis. It can operate both as a general task
force and through a number of subcommittees based on
the needs of particular situations. For example, the
congregation gathers for worship each Sunday; so
someone needs to hand out bulletins, show worshipers
to their seats, and do other work for the comfort of the
people. Therefore, ushers are needed. Likewise, music
expressed through choir, organ, and congregation is
called for; so there must be materials to use and
personnel to use them. Thus, a music committee is
required. Then, the beauty of a sanctuary is enhanced
by the loveliness of flowers, but flowers do not by
themselves march into church. They must be brought
in and arranged. So a flower committee comes into

being. And then there are the occasions of baptism and the Lord's Supper. Baptismal robes do not appear as if by magic, nor does bread upon the Communion table. Someone must do the work of preparation. So there comes into being the ordinance committee. Other task forces or committees relating to worship may be developed as need requires. Likewise, they may be discarded if and when the demand disappears.

The Worship Committee should consist of a chairperson elected by the congregation and at least four members selected by the chairperson and approved by the council or deacons. Each of the four members will have responsibility for one of the subcommittees and will select such helpers as needed. Additional members of the committee may be added as the size and special needs of the congregation demand.

Meetings of the general committee ought to be held once a month and those of the subcommittees as needed. In addition, frequent conferences with the pastor surely will arise. Such conferences may be brief and informal.

DUTIES

Items of concern for the general committee involve such factors as the arrangement and order of the sanctuary and narthex (including their neatness and comfort), arranging for choral and congregational music, checking on bulletins, conferring with the pastor on sermon topics and devotional themes and

with the choir director and organist on music. To be
sure, pastor and music leader are usually professional
people and are trained in their work; but input is
needed to aid them in making their best judgments. A
pastor who is guided in preaching solely by the reaction
received at the door after service is limiting the possible
feedback. Since preaching is one of the basic tasks of the
ministry, it needs to be done well; and it cannot be done
well unless there is calm and reasoned evaluation
received from the hearers. One way this can be
accomplished satisfactorily is through a yearly conference with the worship committee on possible homiletic
themes for the coming year and by an occasional review
of reaction during the year. Pulpit supplies, guest
preachers, and the leadership in music are to be selected
in mutual consultations with the pastor. How many
times churches have fallen into the pit of chaos because
a pastor brought in a guest speaker without conferring
with some official body, or the deacons announced a
visiting minister without consulting the pastor! When
the church is without pastoral or musical leadership,
the Worship Committee will arrange for these vacancies to be filled temporarily in the case of the pulpit and
permanently in the instance of the organ or the choir.

The *subcommittee of ushers* will be under the general
direction of the Worship Committee, and its chairperson will be a member of the Worship Committee.
Ushers will be present at all general worship services of

the church. Their role will be that of host and hostess, making sure that each worshiper is comfortably cared for. This may involve the giving of directions to the coat room (directions to the rest rooms should be indicated so clearly that strangers are not forced to ask), the distribution of bulletins as well as printed announcements and hymnbooks, the seating of worshipers, the control of lighting, the regulation of temperature, the welcoming of latecomers, and otherwise serving as a "bridge" between the world and the sanctuary. At least one usher should be on duty at all times during worship for the purpose of responding to emergencies (people sometimes faint, phones sometimes ring, etc.). Ushers and greeters, who are a part of the evangelistic team, have different functions and should not be confused.

The *subcommittee on music* will be under the general direction of the Worship Committee, and its chairperson will be a member of the Worship Committee. This subcommittee should be composed of a chairperson, one member of the choir, and two members from the congregation. In consultation with the choir director and/or organist, they will be responsible for selecting the special music throughout the year. The choir director may order the music and supplies that have been approved by this subcommittee. The pastor will usually select the hymns to be used in the regular worship services of the church as well as plan the general order of service. The choir director in consultation with the choir members will be responsible for scheduling special music during the months when (and if) the choir does not sing regularly. In the case of multiple choirs, adjustments in these suggestions can be made readily. (See Appendix B for sample guidelines for the music leadership.)

The *subcommittee on flowers* and other decorations will be under the general supervision of the Worship Committee, and its chairperson will be a member of the Worship Committee. A means of enlisting donors of flowers for the beautification of the sanctuary should be devised by this subcommittee (a chart on the church bulletin board is one way). Recognition of those making floral donations may be made through the weekly calendar. Either those donating flowers or the Fellowship Committee will usually be responsible for the disposition of the floral arrangements after the service. Preferably these will be given to people in the hospital or confined to their homes.

The *ordinance subcommittee* will be under the general supervision of the Worship Committee, and its chairperson will be a member of that committee. This subcommittee will be responsible for the obtaining, preparation, and distribution of the elements for the Lord's Supper and for the arrangements for baptism. This work will involve the bread and wine (grape juice) for Communion, the washing of glasses (the use of throwaway cups eliminates this), the polishing of the silver, and the washing and ironing of the linen. The provision of robes for baptismal candidates and the assisting of candidates and the pastor at the time of baptism are important tasks of this committee, also.

In regard to the serving of Communion, the church needs to decide several questions. Shall only deacons or members of the church board be assigned this task? Shall women who are members of the diaconate serve as well as men? (Among the biblical texts which churches may wish to study in this regard is Romans 16:1-2 [RSV]. Here, Paul commends Phoebe to the saints in Rome and observes that she was an officer of the church at Cenchreae. The Greek word used here is *diákonon* which is commonly translated "deacon.") Whatever the decision, the ordinance subcommittee is to be certain that the roster of servers is complete and that the servers are ready for their work. Many churches also have found it expedient to have a training session for servers occasionally so that the work may proceed smoothly and in a dignified manner.

Of course, in addition to the Sunday morning worship service, there will be, in all likelihood, other worship opportunities in the life of the church. Some of these will involve private and/or family devotions. Literature and direction will be needed here. Some worship experiences may take the form of home prayer and Bible study groups. Then, there may also be opportunity to use religious drama, Christian cinema, special speakers, and visiting choirs or music groups. These activities are all within the province of the Worship Committee (sometimes in cooperation with other task forces, such as evangelism or Christian education). All this is done that God may be praised, his Son honored, and his Spirit released.

Chapter 8

The Personnel Committee

It cannot be stressed too strongly that the primary work of a church lies in the development of persons. In other words, the business of the church is people. But the human personality is a most complex and sensitive organism, involving physical, mental, and spiritual elements. A new member of the church, whether coming by the transfer of letter from another congregation or by profession of faith and baptism, enters somewhat as an alien element into an already established society. To fit in and to be fitted into this new order, to make the contribution of one's talents, and to allow others to contribute to the newcomer take conscious effort on the part of both newcomer and congregation. Then, there is the continuing need to minister to each of the members of the congregation as he or she experiences the vicissitudes of life. At these points, the Personnel Committee accepts its charge.

OBJECTIVES

"Koinonia" is a precious word in Christian thought. It comes from the New Testament Greek and means a holding in common or a partnership or a mutual participation. It means: something belonging to several persons (Acts 2:44), to become a sharer in (Romans 15:27), and something of aid or relief (Hebrews 13:16). Thus, the objective of the Personnel Committee is the development and maintenance of the spirit of Christian partnership among the members of the congregation. This is to be done by the establishment and maintenance of means for the free flowing of communion among the members. Such communion is to be done to the end that each may fulfill his or her responsibility before God.

Some churches are little more than preaching stations for learned and articulate ministers. Others provide little more than opportunities for great music to be sung or played. In such cases, it would be very proper to call the place of assembly an "auditorium," that is, a room where things are heard. But the Christian church is a "sanctuary," a place where God is worshiped, hungry souls are fed, the hurt are given healing, the humble are ennobled, and the haughty are made humble. The Personnel Committee enters here.

Its task is to ascertain the needs of each member and to bring the forces of the church to bear upon those needs. All this is done that the believers "may grow up into him in all things, which is the head, even Christ" (Ephesians 4:15).

ORGANIZATION

Responsibility for the formulation and execution of the personnel program should be vested in a committee composed of a chairperson and at least one committee member for every twelve resident families of the church. Each member of the committee can then be assigned one group of families. This may be done on an alphabetical basis, a geographical basis, or some other organizing factor. Sometimes special care will need to be exercised in the assignment of particular families, but this should pose no overriding barrier. A member or a family with whom no one in the committee is able to communicate perhaps ought not be in the church at all. The limit of twelve member families is based on the experience that few lay people have the time to become satisfactorily acquainted with and adequately minister to more than this number.

DUTIES

The function of this committee through its several members is to visit all members of the church, any who may be ill, out of harmony with their families or their church, any who may be in want, any who may be in need of counsel, any who may be lax in their attendance at public worship. Such activities as the distribution of devotional literature, the expression of condolence at the time of grief, the notification of the members regarding special events in the congregation may be considered proper responsibilities of the committee. In pursuance of these duties, the committee will administer the fellowship fund usually received as the Communion offering. Since emergency situations arise from time to time, the pastor should be given the right to respond promptly as wisdom decrees. Some limitation of charitable donations might be established, but both flexibility and the capacity to respond to need ought to be provided.

Some churches have found it helpful to review the church roll once a year. At this session, the name of every member will be read in the committee meeting, and some consensus will be reached concerning each. In a small congregation, this task can be accomplished in one session. In larger churches, the job will take longer. But such review should not be neglected. People are very sensitive and susceptible to all sorts of influences. Christians are no exceptions. Hurts that are not recognized promptly and given healing may grow to such an extent that cure may become difficult if not impossible. Haughtiness reached through pride or achievement may become unbounded and leave its possessor worthless as a witness. The believer is not immune to the effects and forces of the world; but with the support of the Holy Spirit within, the comfort and counsel of Christian friends without, and the ever-present and protective power of Christ round and about, victory can be achieved. It is the place and purpose of the Personnel Committee to supply that "comfort and counsel of Christian friends." To be sure, this is a part of the discipleship call of all followers of Jesus, but experience tells only too plainly that what is everybody's business quickly becomes nobody's business. Then, too, it may be said that this care is the pastor's job. However, he or she has only so much time and so much energy. Furthermore, there is a tendency to keep some things from the pastor. People will tell their friends, their physician, or even a visiting evangelist their problems, but seldom their pastor. They want the minister to see them as they appear in church on Sunday—all clean and scrubbed and filled with goodness. This, of course, is a false front; and for progress to be made in holy living, reality must be faced. The members of the Personnel Committee, living as they do as laymen and laywomen, often are able to achieve a contact that would be forbidden to the minister. With good judgment these committee members will help the pastor know the congregation better and so be able to serve more effectively.

In the case of members whose active relationship to

the church has lapsed, the committee may want to recommend that their names be placed on an inactive list or dropped from the church roll, as the policy of the church may dictate.

Chapter 9

The Christian Education Committee

The Christian church from the beginning has been committed to the work of instructing its initiates and members in the faith. Jesus had the Twelve. These, in turn, were to teach others. Paul wrote, "And God hath set some in the church, first apostles, secondarily prophets, thirdly teachers . . ." (1 Corinthians 12:28). With the rapid spread of Christianity in the early centuries and multitudes of converts coming from paganism, baptism was preceded by instruction and a period of probation.[1] Later, schools arose in connection with cathedrals. Then came the Reformation which demanded a knowledgeable constituency, and education grew accordingly. Finally, in the early years of the

[1] See Kenneth Scott Latourette, *A History of Christianity* (London: Eyre & Spottiswoode Limited, 1953), p. 195.

nineteenth century, the need of religious education for all became apparent, and the Sunday school movement was underway. Sometimes the approach was a simple one designed for the telling of Bible stories and introducing the children to Christ. At other times, there was a great effort expended in the development of a sophisticated curricula with age group differentials and broad theological content. It was hoped that the varied means and methods were suited to the period and to the persons concerned. Certainly, there is a continuing need to assist believers in apprehending a knowledge of God. In the local church, this is the task of the committee on Christian education.

OBJECTIVES

The objective of the Christian Education Committee is the training of persons in the congregation and constituency in the Word of God and in his way. The means and manner of this task in the local church is to be decided by the committee after prayerful study, research, and testing. The curriculum ought to be under constant and consistent review. What doctrinal teachings should be emphasized? It should be obvious that not all doctrines of such a well-developed faith as Christianity can be stressed at once. An examination of various texts on Christian education may be made for the purpose of familiarizing the committee with general objectives as stated by denominational and other publishing houses. In addition, handbooks on theology will prove useful to be sure that a full structure of Christian thought is being presented and with the emphasis that the local church deems right and proper for its particular situation. Handed-down objectives often fit no more comfortably than handed-down clothing. Certainly churches will want to have some teaching on God, humanity, sin, salvation, revelation, Jesus Christ, the Holy Spirit, Christian life and action, and last things. Many other items could be added to this list, of course, but the Christian Education Committee must frequently ask this question: "What is crucially important in the lives of the scholars in our school that is not being taught elsewhere?" Religion is not the fourth "r" in most schools of general education, but it is important and should be taught somewhere.

ORGANIZATION

Responsibility for the formulation and execution of the program of Christian education should be vested in a committee composed of the chairperson, divisional leaders for children, youth, adults, and leadership education, and the pastor. The divisional leaders will have as large or as small a staff of teachers and workers as need and opportunity demand.

DUTIES

The function of the Christian Education

Committee is to provide for activities such as church school, the youth fellowship, special educational programs, vacation church school, leadership training, camps and conferences, weekday religious education, and discipleship classes. The duty of each of the four divisions is to plan and administer the total Christian education program within its respective field. Plans are to be submitted to the general committee for discussion and approval or modification and referred back to the divisions for action.

The choice of curriculum materials is a heavy responsibility. Many churches regularly turn to their own denominational publishing houses for material. Usually, two or three different types of material are offered so that some choice is offered the local church. However, the composition of individual congregations varies so widely and situations are so different that some churches choose an amalgam of courses or even write their own. When this is done, extra care needs to be taken to provide balance and wholeness.

Of unusual importance in the Christian education program is the recognition that the mobility rate in most communities is high. Therefore, the church educational program cannot be built on the premise that its scholars will be present for a several-year cycle of studies. Indeed, attendance from week to week often varies so much that many miss crucially important items of truth unless they are frequently repeated. This is a factor which calls for simplicity of curriculum.

Simplicity of curriculum is also demanded by the teachers. Much fine material has been produced that has not been enthusiastically accepted by the churches because it requires a professional level of instructorship not often available to the local church.

Maintaining and increasing enrollment is also a subject of prime importance to the committee on Christian education. It used to be said that the Sunday school was the chief feeder for the church—and statistics were offered to prove it. If this axiom continues to be true, the churches are in deep trouble. A glance at the annual report of a large state association of churches shows that Sunday school enrollment runs about one-third that of church membership. The lack of growth potential here is obvious. Thus, the Christian Education Committee will work closely with the Evangelism Committee in recruitment and with the Personnel Committee in conservation of membership.

Chapter 10

The Property Committee

A congregation needs a place to meet and to pursue its corporate life. Usually this means an edifice of considerable size and worth. In one state association, there are 216 member churches with a total valuation of $54,000,000. This results in an average property worth of $250,000 each. Some properties, of course, are large and commodious structures with a value much beyond that; others are simple edifices costing much less. In one cluster of 15 churches, there were 6 valued at less than a quarter of a million dollars and 9 at more than that sum. Of the 6, the lowest figure was $100,000. Even this is a large amount of treasure. Custodians of such assets have no minor responsibility. Church buildings in this regard are no different from dwelling houses or business blocks. Regular maintenance is required, or else deterioration will quickly gain its harvest of neglect. Herein lies the work of the Property Committee.

OBJECTIVES

The detail with which God instructed the children of Israel in the construction of the tabernacle in the wilderness (Exodus 26; 27; 35–38) and the explanation regarding its care (Numbers 18:1-7) were given so explicitly that the significance of the structure was self-evident: This was to be God's particular and peculiar dwelling place among his children. His tent would be in the midst of theirs. It was to be beautifully arranged and richly done. Nothing cheap or shoddy was to go into its construction. Likewise, it was to be maintained as fitting its purpose. Later, when the Hebrews had a permanent country and capital, the same care and keeping were given to the temple (1 Kings 5:1-6:38; 7:13-9:9, 25). It was the center of Hebrew history and hope, and they treated it accordingly. When the temple was not properly used, the occupants paid accordingly: Jesus cleansed it! (see Matthew 21:12-13).

The New Testament church does not look upon its buildings with such reverence. It realizes its temple is elsewhere and is not made of wood or stone or mortar. The temple of the church lies, first, in the bodies of believers (1 Corinthians 6:19) and, ultimately, in heaven (Revelation 7:15). However, Christians from the beginning have treated their public places of meeting with God with care and concern. This has been done both as a witness to what the building represents and as an educational tool for the worshipers.

The objective of the Property Committee, therefore, is to have an edifice and grounds which will honor God and be of service to people. Thus, the building needs to be of sound construction, attractively and adequately appointed, decently maintained, and properly prepared for worship and service.

ORGANIZATION

Responsibility for the care and maintenance of the church property will be vested in a committee composed of a chairperson and at least two other members. Institutions with extensive grounds, a parsonage, summer camps, and other assets will probably want a number of subcommittees, with each assigned to a particular division of the work.

DUTIES

Many churches have either a full- or a part-time employee serving as custodian. The Property Committee is still responsible either to do the following tasks itself or see that such tasks are accomplished: the building is cleaned and heated/cooled for services; the building is repaired; the plumbing works; the lights operate; the musical instruments (piano, organ) are tuned and in working order; the lawn is cut and cared for; the rubbish is disposed of; the trees and shrubs are trimmed and protected; janitorial supplies are obtained; snow is removed from walks, driveways, and parking lot; flower beds are planted and kept free of weeds; time clocks are set; signs are painted and kept up to date; offices are maintained; and the whole property is kept useful and in order. While the minister, of course, will be a member of this committee, it should not be a part of the clerical responsibility to dust the pews, unlock the church, fix the plumbing when it blocks, or clean out the baptistry. Pastors often do all these things and much more, but it is to the shame of the church when this is so. The pastor may find it convenient or expedient to engage in these activities, but the involvement ought to be no more than that of any other member of the congregation, and it should be considered as an emergency measure.

In the case of a request for use of the church for weddings, social events, or otherwise, it is usually the policy to make no charge when the request is made by church members for ecclesiastically related activities. The matter may be cleared between the pastor and the property chairperson. For requests made by nonchurch members and/or for requests made for nonecclesiastical activities (e.g., Scouts, clubs, nursery school, community gatherings, etc.), it may be wise for the property chairperson to bring the matter to the church board for action and for the setting of a fee or donation. Some activities and some groups do not fit the cultural image which the congregation wishes to maintain in the community.

Because maintenance needs the wisdom of the user, the Property Committee will find it helpful to cooperate with the social chairperson in the cleaning and upkeep of the church kitchen, with the chairperson of worship in the care of the musical instruments, with the chairperson of Christian education in the cleaning and care of the classrooms and other church property under educational use, and with the church clerk in maintaining an ordered and efficient office. If a parsonage is owned by the church, then the upkeep of this also becomes the responsibility of the Property Committee, cooperating, of course, with the parsonage resident.

The Property Committee is neither the board of trustees nor the board of the church recognized by the state for official business. The legal authority remains with the trustees if a three- or four-board system is followed or with the church board or diaconate if a one-board arrangement is designed.

Chapter 11

The Stewardship Committee

The Bible has much to say about stewardship, and, from the practical standpoint, unless this area of responsibility is fulfilled well, failure as a church is imminent. A church that neglects to respond to God's grace with reasonable stewardship is doomed. Fortunately, churches today understand this commission much better than they did in some periods of history.

The ideology of Christian stewardship may be more fully understood from the following points:

1. God expects us to understand that he is the source of all things. He gave us the world, our life, and the environment for life; he gave us the Word, our direction, and the enablement of our direction; he gave us heaven and the essentials to enter and to enjoy (James 1:17).

2. God expects us to avail ourselves of the gifts which have been given. These include: the earth and the things of the earth (Genesis 1:28), the kingdom and the things of the kingdom (Mark 12:28-34), the Spirit and the things of the Spirit (Galatians 5:22-23).

3. God expects us to share our gifts (Luke 12:42-43). The tenth of the harvest belongs to God, according to the Old Testament (Leviticus 27:30), an idea which Jesus approves (Matthew 23:23) and pursues to the point of the sacrifice of all possessions (Luke 21:3-4). Through the doctrine of the sabbath, one-seventh of our time belongs to God also (Exodus 20:8-11).

4. God expects to receive an accounting from every person at the end of time (Romans 14:12).

5. We will be judged at the final review according to the light we have had and how we have used our gifts (Matthew 25:14-30).

6. We may find the central interest of our lives by locating the site of our treasure (Luke 12:34).

7. We who name the name of Jesus have the responsibility of carrying on God's mission and of supporting those who do (Mark 16:15; 1 Timothy 5:17-18).

OBJECTIVES

One practical method of giving substance to these points in stewardship is through the budget system of weekly or monthly pledged gifts. As Paul wrote to the Corinthians, "Upon the first day of the week let every one of you lay by him in store, as God hath prospered him, that there be no gatherings when I come" (1 Corinthians 16:2). The combination of ideas in this verse is impressive. The giving is to be done on the first day of each week, presumably in connection with the worship service at which God's name is praised and God's gospel is preached. From the first, giving has been an important part of worship. Regularity also is enhanced, which is a constant reminder that we "are not our own, that we have been bought with a price." Furthermore, the giving is to be done proportionally. God does not bless all alike. Some can sing; some can preach; some can evangelize; some can safely venture into distant places; some can organize business profitably; some can administer; some can teach. So it becomes the objective of the Stewardship Committee to search out the gifts of all and prepare challenging opportunities to which members of the congregation may respond. In other words, stewardship involves more than money. It embraces time and talent as well as treasure. To this end, therefore, the Stewardship Committee will seek to apprise the members of the congregation and friends of the wide variety of needs and opportunities which the church offers through its various programs and to which they may respond.

ORGANIZATION

The Stewardship Committee should be composed of a chairperson, elected by the church, the financial secretary, and the treasurer. Additional members may be invited by the chairperson to cooperate in special projects and campaigns.

DUTIES

It is the function of the Stewardship Committee to plan and prepare the financial budget for the church. This is done, of course, in cooperation with the church board. The Stewardship Committee seeks budget needs from the various program committees of the board, reviews these against anticipated receipts from the church, exercises judgment as to the amount by which members may be expected to increase their commitment, and then puts together a total from the sum of the parts which may be presented to the board for examination and adjustment, if necessary, and then to the congregation for adoption. The chief means for raising the budget may vary. One common way is through an Every Member Financial Canvass. Typically, the order of events for the Stewardship Committee might be: in September of each year gather data for budget needs; in early October put these requests together in a challenge budget for review by the board; in late October present a proposed budget to the church; in early November train those assisting with the Canvass; and in late November hold the Canvass with the climax coming on the Sunday before Thanksgiv-

ing. In December, the results of the Canvass may be
weighed against the proposed budget; and from these
factors, plus information regarding income which
reaches the church from other sources, a realistic budget
may be prepared to present to the church for adoption at
the annual meeting in January. As local, national, or
denominational situations change, such a schedule
would be subject to modification by the committee.

From time to time during the year, the Stewardship
Committee will seek to review the giving of the
congregation. If there is a decline, individually or
collectively, the financial secretary will wish to report
this to the committee for action deemed appropriate by
the group. The committee members may handle the
matter themselves, refer it to the Personnel Committee,
inform the pastor, or seek the judgment of the board. In
all this, the committee will remain discreet, but it must
not remain dumb. The financial pulse of an individual
or a church is one of the most important indicators of
spiritual vitality. The Stewardship Committee will also
keep alert to new members joining the church and will
see that each is supplied with a box of envelopes and has
an opportunity to make a pledge after learning of the
budgetary program.

A second function of the Stewardship Committee is
the gathering of information regarding the abilities,
interests, and talents of the congregation in other than
financial ways. This may be done through the

development and maintenance of a Service File or Talent Ballot. Cards can be obtained or made which list the wide choice of activity and service opportunities offered by the church and inviting the individual members to indicate past service and/or present interest. This file can be of great assistance to the pastor and to the nominating committee as they seek to fill the various offices in the church organization. A perusal of this file would also be helpful to the several committee chairpersons as they look for people to occupy the several posts in the given departments. Such a survey need not be taken every year, but on occasion it may be taken in conjunction with the Every Member Financial Canvass, and it should be kept up to date by the Stewardship Committee chairperson. The file may be kept in such a place as the chairperson determines best, but one such place would be the church office.

Chapter 12

The Missions Committee

The Psalmist said, "Declare his glory among the heathen, his wonders among all people" (Psalm 96:3). Jesus said, "Go ye into all the world, and preach the gospel to every creature" (Mark 16:15). Empowered by the Holy Spirit, the early disciples obeyed, beginning "in Jerusalem, and in all Judaea, and in Samaria, and unto the uttermost part of the earth" (Acts 1:8). To a greater or lesser extent, his continuing disciples have followed the same instructions and to that measure have achieved victory for Christ.

OBJECTIVES

This Great Commission has never been abrogated; it is still the "marching orders" of the church. Some authorities state that "evangelism and missions are almost the same"[1] but find the distinction in the fact that "the church commissions some of its number to represent it in proclaiming the gospel beyond its immediate locality."[2] While this may be so, it would perhaps be more helpful to view the matter ecclesiologically. Thus, evangelism would have as its goal the building of the body of the local church and missions the building of the body of the church universal. The work of missions should be free from all sense of enlarging the membership of the local congregation, while the work of evangelism is closely related to the growth of the congregation. Missions has as its focal point that which is outside the immediate church family. Furthermore, its concerns must be the whole person: physical, mental, moral, spiritual. In the nearby neighborhood or in distant parts, where there is need, there missions finds its opportunity.

ORGANIZATION

Responsibility for the formulation and execution of the program of expressing Christian care and concern to those beyond the perimeter of the given congregation may be vested in a committee composed of the chairperson and at least two other members at large. In addition, the presidents of the men's and

[1] Norman H. Maring and Winthrop S. Hudson, *A Baptist Manual of Polity and Practice* (Valley Forge: Judson Press, 1963), p. 118.
[2] *Ibid.*

women's fellowships (assuming the existence of such organizations in the church) or their representatives should be full members of the committee.

DUTIES

The function of this committee is to prepare a budget composed of items for missionary support. At least 75 percent (or whatever percentage seems reasonable) of the missionary support items budgeted should be designated for programs sponsored by the denomination to which the local church belongs or by one of its affiliates or constituent bodies. Should other items of a missionary character be presented to the church beyond this budget, the committee may wish to review the merits of the case and recommend appropriate action to the congregation. It is also to be the duty of this committee to foster the education of the congregation and its various departments for the understanding and support of the mission program. This may involve distributing promotional literature, making oral and written announcements to the congregation, presenting audiovisual programs, arranging schools of missions, bringing in special speakers, maintaining a missions bulletin board in the vestibule, supervising the missions bookshelf, gathering and forwarding food and clothing, corresponding with those on mission fields, and serving as liaison between the local church and the denominational boards of national and international ministries to facilitate relationships.

In pursuance of its duties, the committee may find it helpful to sponsor prayer fellowships with regard to problems and opportunities on the mission fields. It will cooperate with the Worship and Christian Education Committees when mutually helpful.

Further, there is more to the Christian mission than the preaching of the gospel and the instruction in the way thereof in distant parts. The local church needs to become alert to moral issues affecting the community, drawing the attention of the congregation to these matters and suggesting means for expressing Christian social concern. The church that does not make itself heard and felt in the midst of the community in which it lives is forfeiting a measure of its obligation and determining its death. There is more to the gospel than social action, but there is not less. It was said of Jesus that he "went about doing good" (Acts 10:38). He healed "all manner of sickness" (Matthew 4:23). He cleansed the temple of its corruption (Luke 19:45-46). He fed the hungry (Matthew 14:19-20). He commissioned his followers to do likewise as well as to clothe the naked, give shelter to the stranger and refreshment to the thirsty, and visit those in prison (Matthew 25:35-36). The penalty for not doing such is dire. It is exclusion from the kingdom (Matthew 25:26-30).

Thus, the Missions Committee will seek areas of service in the community and in the world at large. The variety of such service is great. An emergency food bank may be established. Religious services may be held at the county jail. Clothing may be collected for a city mission or for Church World Service. Studies may be made of impending legislation which may foster, or hinder, the moral tone of the city, state, or nation, and lobby efforts may be organized or letters written to those in government. Since all problems cannot be faced effectively at all times, selections must be made for emphasis. From time to time, it may be helpful to compile a list of problem areas and select two or three to emphasize each year. For example, a catalog might include issues such as the use of alcoholic beverages, church and state, education, the elderly, the environment, gambling, health, human rights, hunger, labor-management relations, obscenity, pornography, poverty, race relations, safety, Sunday observance, the use of tobacco, violence, and war and peace. The occasion of time, need, and moral climate will help the process of choice. In short, the gospel must be freed to do its work upon individuals collectively as well as upon individuals separately.

Chapter 13

The Social Committee

Early in the story of God's people, they were bid to receive strangers, for, says the Bible, "[they] were strangers in the land of Egypt." Also, it might be added, travelers had to cross barren land devoid of water, food, or shelter. The accommodating household was often the only place of refuge. Later on, the early Christians were as much strangers in an alien land as was Ruth, the Moabitess, in Judea. The first followers of Jesus found great comfort not only in the sharing of their faith but also in the sharing of their food. The upper room was not only a place for prayer, but it was also a place for eating. The meals served were hearty in nature and were supplied by the contributions of all. So remarkable were they in the fashion of communal dining that they became known as "love feasts" and were an early mark of the church. For a time, these occasions were the only meals for Christians and some—forgetful of both manners and morality—gorged themselves to the deprivation of others. This sad sinfulness brought about the fullest directive that we have concerning the observance of the Lord's Supper (1 Corinthians 11:17-30).

Jesus' readiness to attend a wedding (John 2:1-10) and a great feast (Luke 5:29) and to have dinner with a tax collector (Luke 19:5) indicates the importance of hospitality for growth in the church. Sociability and spirituality are not far apart in the English dictionary; neither are they greatly separated in the Lord's lexicon. Still they are distinct. It should be emphasized that the Social Committee is not to be confused with the Personnel Committee. Both labor in the area of Christian fellowship, but they toil with different tools. The one uses the worship service, the prayer meeting, and the counseling room to advance its purpose. The other uses a breakfast, a dinner, a coffee hour, or a party. In each case, human effort and ingenuity are required. In both instances, the advancement of the kingdom of God in the life of the individual is the goal.

ORGANIZATION

Responsibility for the formulation and execution of the program of Christian sociality and hospitality can be given to a committee composed of the chairperson and at least two other active members.

DUTIES

The function of this committee is to provide for the social activities of the church. This involves the establishment of opportunities for the individual members to develop the sense of association for common cause and in response to common need. The aim of this committee remains the same as that of the other groups in the church—to aid a person or persons to live in unity and harmony with others and with God. The means used by the Social Committee are different, however. These involve the arrangement for church dinners, provision for luncheons for various working groups at the church, direction of wedding receptions for members of the congregation when asked, and the sponsorship of church socials, receptions, entertainments, and parties. Coffee hours after the worship service or between Sunday school and church have been found to be useful and popular in many congregations.

In the course of these activities, the Social Committee will be responsible for the care of the church kitchen and its equipment and appliances, the dining room and its furnishings, and other social parlors. They will see that neatness and cleanliness prevail in those areas at all times and direct those who use the facilities to act accordingly. Upon the occasion of pastoral receptions or other social events of general interest, the Social

Committee will have the overall responsibility. Organized Sunday school classes, youth groups, men's and women's fellowships, and other organizations which use church property and equipment for meals, parties, and the like will find it helpful to inform the Social Committee of their activities so that coordination of effort may be strong.

It should be emphasized that the Social Committee, like other committees, is both a management and a labor force. The measure to which each of these expressions of stewardship is given emphasis depends upon the local committee and the local situation. Responsibility for the social life of the congregation is placed here, but that is not to say that all, or even any, of the toiling in the kitchen is to be done by the committee members. Delegation is not only proper, but it is also often wise.

Part Three:

Coordination and Administration

Chapter 14

The General Officers

In the military, one speaks of "line" and "staff" officers. Staff officers deal with the general, internal, and/or overall operations of the organization, and line officers have responsibility for actually carrying out the plans. Church officers may be divided somewhat in the same way. Following this approach, there are four general church lay officials who function as staff officers. The titles may vary, but the commonly used ones are moderator, clerk, financial secretary, and treasurer. Each or any of these, of course, may have as many assistants as the situation requires.

THE MODERATOR

In times past, the pastor usually was understood to be the presiding officer at the church business meetings. More recently, congregations have chosen to select lay people to serve in this position. The arguments for this increasingly common position are at least two-fold: (1) The pastor is freed from some administrative duties, and (2) there is more liberty for the minister to participate in the discussion as a resource person. In either case—whether the pastor or a lay person serves as moderator—the task of the moderator remains much the same.

Objectives

Since a church following the congregational polity makes basic decisions through the parliamentary process in a church meeting, the church needs to have a presiding officer who can elicit an accurate reading of the corporate mind and maintain coordination of responsibility among the members of the church board or diaconate with the congregation at large. As chairperson of both the congregation and the diaconate or board, the moderator occupies a unique position for ministry in the life of the church.

Responsibilities

In the fulfillment of duties, the moderator presides at all meetings of the congregation and diaconate or board. (In the case of the moderator's absence and in an emergency, the pastor or someone selected by the assembly may preside.) The moderator should know and practice the proper means of conducting meetings. Among congregationally oriented denominations, *Robert's Rules of Order* and other commonly accepted manuals in use, such as *The Star Book for Ministers* by Hiscox, *A Baptist Manual of Polity and Practice* by Maring and Hudson, and *The Church Business Meeting* by Merrill, are valuable handbooks.[1] The moderator is also responsible for maintaining coordination among the members of the official board or diaconate by assisting the pastor in the indoctrination of new officers as to their duties and superintending the orderly transfer of incumbency, including program and property. This would involve briefing new officers on the continuing program of their particular committeeship and the conveyance of church property such as keys, records, and other items. In the conduct of meetings of the board or diaconate, the moderator will allow much flexibility in parliamentary procedure and may freely discuss issues without leaving the chair. In the congregational meeting, however, a more detached

[1] Henry M. Robert, *Robert's Rules of Order Revised: 75th Anniversary Edition* (New York: William Morrow & Co., Inc., 1971); Edward T. Hiscox, *The Star Book for Ministers*, revised edition (Valley Forge: Judson Press, 1967); Norman H. Maring and Winthrop S. Hudson, *A Baptist Manual of Polity and Practice* (Valley Forge: Judson Press, 1963); Maring and Hudson, *A Short Baptist Manual of Polity and Practice* (Valley Forge: Judson Press, 1965); and R. Dale Merrill, *The Church Business Meeting* (Valley Forge: Judson Press, 1968).

position should be maintained. The aim always is to be sure the facts are adequately stated, the alternatives clearly defined, and the decision understood. In achieving these goals, four principles will be found helpful:

1. Courtesy and justice for all.
2. Consider one thing at a time.
3. The minority must be heard.
4. The majority must prevail.[2]

In further ordering of duties, the moderator may be considered the liaison person between the congregation and pastor for mutual encouragement, counsel, and direction. In addition, the moderator will be welcomed at the various committee meetings of the church, may participate in discussion, but will remain without vote in those sessions. In short, the moderator may be considered the lay leader of the church.

CLERK

The keeping of records is a very important task in God's work. The prominence given to family or genealogical lists is marked in both the Old and New Testaments. By this means, inheritance, marriage, land redemption, and temple service were managed (Ezra

[2] Marguerite Grumme, *Basic Principles of Parliamentary Law and Protocol* (Old Tappan, N.J.: Fleming H. Revell Co., 1963), p. 7; quoted in Merrill, *op. cit.*, p. 15.

2:59-63). Long before the children of Israel reached the Promised Land, Moses was commissioned by God to take a census (Numbers 1:2). The practice of maintaining family lists continued over the centuries and has been helpful in many aspects of biblical study. The task of the clerk in the contemporary church is different. Births, marriages, wills, deaths, and burials are carefully recorded by secular agencies. The church clerk is called upon to maintain records of baptisms, church and Sunday school attendance, and decisions of the congregation.

Objectives

The function of the church clerk is to keep accurate records of membership and congregational decisions. The better those records are, the less chance the church has of taking an ill-advised action. When decisions are made upon the basis of what someone thinks happened instead of what is clearly recorded in the minutes of the congregation, the foundation of further trouble is laid.

Duties

The duties of the church clerk may vary from church to church. In larger churches some of the tasks listed here may be handled by the church secretary or other persons. Generally, the clerk is responsible for keeping the records of the church. This involves taking the minutes of board and congregational meetings and presenting them for oral report or visual reading at the next session of the particular body. At a minimum, such accounts should note the time of beginning and the time of adjournment, the members present (if the board) and the number present (if the congregation); the presiding officer should be named, and the clerk should inscribe his or her name at the close of the report. The minutes should also state each motion made, together with the mover and seconder of the proposed matter. The motion should be presented in written form in the meeting. If orally stated, the clerk should ascertain whether or not the record of the motion is correct before action is taken. These minutes should be placed in a book for safekeeping so that in time to come (either short or long) ready reference may be made to them. It might be well for the records to be kept in annual volumes or notebooks and at the close of each year an index of the crucial items be compiled. This can be of great service in years to come when the record of particular actions is sought. Furthermore, in addition to current files, those of all former years should be in the custody of the clerk. These past files need to be kept in a place where they will be safe from destruction and deterioration and where they may be researched without difficulty. It is also the responsibility of the retiring clerk to inform his or her successor, the pastor, and the moderator of the location of past files and to transfer to the successor the current files and records.

The clerk's task is also to keep the membership roll of the church up to date. This will include additions and by what means; deletions and by what manner; name changes because of marriage, along with mate and date noted; and time and place of death, and of burial if it is significant. The manner of maintaining the membership roll should be consistent with that employed in the past unless that method has been hopelessly confusing, in which case a new system may be inaugurated but with full data transferred from the old.

A church may wish to prepare a directory of active resident members and active non-resident members with addresses and telephone numbers for ready reference by all. This directory may also include friends of the church who are not members but who have given indication of interest. The preparation of this list is the responsibility of the Personnel Committee, but the publication would be the business of the clerk.

Many churches have a memorial fund book in which are recorded special gifts—large and small—which have come to the church over the years from devoted members and interested friends. The keeping of this book, or a similar record, might also be the business of the clerk.

Each year, the local association or cluster of churches may desire to have a letter of account from each member church. In this will be reported the significant victories and defeats of the congregation the previous year. Likewise, the state or regional organization usually seeks a full report of the year's activities for its own records and for the national body to which the church belongs. The preparation of these reports, usually in consultation with the pastor, comes within the clerk's portfolio.

The clerk is also the "correspondence officer" of the congregation. In this regard, letters of dismission for those members leaving the church and requests for letter of admission for those coming into the church will be written. Upon occasion, special letters from the congregation will be authorized, such as notes of appreciation, congratulation, or condolence. Copies of these, of course, should be retained with the records. At other times, important items of business correspondence prepared by the clerk on behalf of the congregation will be written. When a new pastor is selected, the official notification will be made in writing by the clerk.

In the organization of responsibility for administration of the church property, the clerk may be accountable for the church office. This will involve both the obtaining and the maintaining of the furniture and equipment, the responsibility for supplies, and the general order of the office and files. Among churches with a paid staff, these responsibilities may be delegated, no doubt.

If it is not possible or expedient for the congregation to have a church historian, it would be well for the clerk to assume such duties in this regard. At a minimum, this would require the saving of the weekly bulletins, the annual reports (if printed or mimeographed), and other booklets of special interest. Identified folders in a file cabinet would be one simple means of receiving and storing this data. At the dissolution of a church or to prevent the loss of valuable records of an old historic congregation, the clerk, upon direction of the church, may wish to transfer the more valuable documents to some local historical repository or to the denomination's national historical society.

FINANCIAL SECRETARY

Many churches, both large and small, have found it expedient to have two financial officers: a treasurer to regulate the outflow of monies and a financial secretary to monitor the income. Such a check-and-balance system helps prevent financial misadventures as well as offers a more equitable arrangement of time demands upon the officers of the church.

Objectives

The task of the financial secretary is to keep a full and accurate record of all monies coming into the treasury of the church. Jesus' parable of the talents indicates the fact that God expects his children to be careful in the administration of his property. The gifts which have been bestowed upon us are to be treated accordingly. They are not to be stored away unused. They are not to be wasted in "riotous living." They are to be used and accounted for. If even the hairs of the head are numbered (Luke 12:7), how much more' our money? God keeps track of what we do with that which is his. So should we. Charles Wesley was in tune with the whole biblical outlook as he wrote,

> And O, thy servant, Lord, prepare
> A strict account to give.

Duties

In the fulfillment of these objectives, the financial secretary receives each year from the members and friends of the congregation the pledges toward the budget. These will be in a book or card file listing the name, address, amount of pledge, and contributor's number. As much as possible, these pledges should be recorded in alphabetical order. The account book should be devised so as to record the yearly total pledge as well as weekly or monthly amounts. Also, provision should be made for the noting of special gifts. The arrangement should be such that at the end of each fiscal year, the summation of each giving unit can be totaled readily. Some may wish to use a loose-leaf binder with quadruplicate sets of report forms whereby at the close of each quarter a statement of standing may be sent to each giver of record with a full report of each gift and the date thereof. Such materials are available from the denominational and other church supply houses. The financial secretary should order these as needed. It is also the duty of the financial secretary to order church envelopes, if such a plan is commended by the congregation. These will be properly inscribed with names of all givers of record for distribution before the first Sunday of each fiscal year. Should a member fall behind in his or her pledge, the financial secretary should inquire discreetly about the situation and, if it seems proper, suggest a readjustment of the pledge. If the member indicates a situation of spiritual maladjustment, such a state ought to be reported to the pastor and the Personnel Committee at once. New members coming into the church during the year should be supplied with information about the church budget, with an opportunity to make a pledge and with a box of envelopes, if that is the method of giving which is followed.

On Sunday, the ushers who collect the offering will transfer it to the custody of the financial secretary. Ideally, the money should be counted by two or more people and that be done before leaving the church. Notations can be made on the envelopes of money contained therein and these envelopes later transferred to the secretary's home or office in order for him or her to enter the gifts into the account book. A deposit slip can be made out, the money placed in a bag furnished by the bank for this purpose, and the deposit made on the way home from church. This procedure is the best one to follow from the standpoint of safety as well as other considerations. However, sometimes in a large church this is not feasible because of the number of envelopes to process, and sometimes in a small church the financial secretary and his or her helpers will have other responsibilities. The solution in this case may be to take the money home, or place it in the night deposit at the bank, for tabulation later. Whatever plan is devised, it should provide for safety.

Reports

The financial secretary should make monthly reports to the board of all monies received and of the standing *vis-à-vis* the budget. At the end of the year, a similar report is due the church. As a member of the Stewardship Committee, the financial secretary may be expected to render exceptional service by advice based on experience. A chart showing how many in the congregation give how much can be very helpful in awakening the church to responsible stewardship.

TREASURER

The treasurer shares with the financial secretary

and the stewardship chairperson the immediate responsibility for the fiscal well-being of the church. The stewardship chairperson is the chief officer of enlistment support, the financial secretary is the overseer of income, while the treasurer is the superintendent of expenditures.

Objectives

Few churches have, and no church should have, an excess of funds. The needs of the world are so great as to preclude the accumulation of a surplus. Therefore, the task of the treasurer usually is a demanding one. This officer stands at the headgate of the treasury and keeps a steady watch upon the inflow and outgo of money. On occasion the treasurer must be a bearer of bad news—alerting the church when expenditures are exceeding income—but such a concern must not be allowed to dominate the aggressive steps in faith of the church. Of course, it goes without saying that the treasurer must be careful and honest in the care of the church's funds and careful for the reputation of the church in the community. This is the Lord's money and this is the Lord's work.

Duties

In the fulfillment of these duties, the treasurer has two chief responsibilities: custodian of liquid assets and paymaster. As custodian, he or she will have the management of the church's money. The contributions, having been banked weekly by the financial secretary or someone designated by him or her, will be reported promptly to the treasurer and so noted in the ledger kept for that purpose. Only the treasurer shall be authorized to draw funds against this account. It may be expedient to have the church authorize more than one name to be valid for the writing of checks, but the issuing of checks should be done only within the realm of the treasurer's responsibility. There should be but one ledger for the entering of deposits and expenditures. There should be but one checkbook and all dispensing of funds be through that book. Separate bank accounts held by a variety of organizations and boards make for fiscal confusion and form an impenetrable barrier in determining the full stewardship accountability of the church.

As paymaster, the treasurer should maintain orderly files for every canceled check and every accompanying bill or voucher. The treasurer should ascertain the validity of every bill before payment by means of a signed voucher from the proper church officer, except for regular expenses such as salaries and utilities. Payment for all special items must be authorized by the board or the church. Even then, frequent brief conferences with the proper officer are in order. Sometimes errors occur in bills, and sometimes employees are due an amount other than the budgeted sum. It is true that the officer responsible for that department in the church should take the initiative in informing the treasurer of any variation, but if both will take the responsibility to check with each other, difficulties can be avoided. Needless to say, to keep the reputation of the church healthy in the community, the treasurer will pay all bills as promptly as funds allow.

Reports

The treasurer should make to the board monthly reports of all monies disbursed and of the standing of each department *vis-à-vis* the budget. At the end of the year, a similar report is due the church. These reports should be of such nature as to be both accurate and to be understood easily by those not accustomed to the reading of balance sheets prepared by accountants. Also, the reports ought to follow a standard format so that although individual office holders may change, the reports will vary only in content. This will allow for valid comparision studies over the year. Furthermore, this format will allow those other than bookkeepers or accountants to serve in the office of treasurer. As a member of the Stewardship Committee, the treasurer will be expected to render advice in budget building and in budget maintenance. (See Appendix C for a sample treasurer's report form.)

Chapter 15

The Pastor

Pastoral leadership was clearly commended in the New Testament. It was stated by the apostle Paul, "And his gifts were that some should be apostles, some prophets, some evangelists, some pastors and teachers" (Ephesians 4:11, RSV). These gifts were for the purpose that believers might be edified, the church be built up, and those being saved be brought into the fellowship. The term used in this instance for "pastor" was translated elsewhere as "shepherd" and was commonly used. From this typology of the shepherd has arisen much of the concept of the pastorate.

POSITION

As shepherd of the flock, the pastor is the overseer of the congregation (Acts 20:28). Many heads mean frustration and chaos. This the New Testament does not ordain. "Obey your leaders and submit to them; for they are keeping watch over your souls, as men who will have to give account. Let them do this joyfully, and not sadly, for that would be of no advantage to you" (Hebrews 13:17, RSV). Such administration must always be done in accordance with the love of Christ, in response to the call of God and in recognition of the autonomy of the local congregation.

The pastor is not the congregation's "hired hand." Much dissatisfaction among church members and much uneasiness among the clergy can be traced to a lack of understanding of the pastoral position. He or she was called of God for service, appointed by God for assignment, and directed for the administration of His work. To the extent that the pastor's ministry is not divinely oriented, the service will be flawed. Likewise, the congregation should not seek its own will, but make every effort to be guided by the Spirit. Action not bathed in prayer is likely to result in unwashed results indeed. The pastor will be, *ex officio*, a member of all boards and committees of the church. In cases of a multiple ministry, specific assignments will be made to the various clergy on the staff. Even so, the senior minister will be briefed on all important issues and will continue to function as overseer.

The modern situation calls for a pastor highly skilled and trained in the arts of administration. The rising level of education among the laity combined with a shorter work week allow more time and more talent to be available for ministry by the members than once was possible. Thus, it is no longer necessary, or even wise, for the pastor to do all of the evangelistic work, all of the visitation of the sick, or all the direction of interest and age-group activities. It is true that pastors *can* work ninety hours a week in these pursuits and that many do, but they ought not to do so. Such overinvolvement on the part of the minister is fair neither to the congregation nor to the parsonage family; the one is being cheated of the opportunity of service and the other of the blessing of a participating parent and mate.

RESPONSIBILITIES

The minister is the chief executive officer of the congregation and the fulfillment of the pastoral office demands many talents skillfully used. The pastor is to equip the saints "for the work of the ministry" and to build up "the body of Christ" (Ephesians 4:12, RSV). Thus the primary role includes: the teaching of disciples, the preaching of the gospel, the counseling of souls, and the administration of the church. In the pursuit of these responsibilities, the minister will find it necessary to prepare carefully and deliver articulately talks and sermons, to attend diligently to the business of the church, to visit faithfully the members whether in sickness or in health, to perform with dignity ceremonial duties such as weddings and funerals, and on occasion to be the representative of the congregation. The pastor will also give attention to the various disciplines of the expression of Christian witness, such as evangelism, social betterment, stewardship, and missions, through example and direction. However, the pastor, while actively participating in these expressions, will seek to be a resource person and stimulator rather than the star performer. He or she will not only be personally involved in the various expressions of witness but will also be devoted to the instruction of others. Division between the arena and the grandstand ought to be reduced as much as possible. The average congregation of twentieth-century Christians usually includes a wide variety of persons with special talent and training. Such skills ought to be used for God, and the minister will seek to encourage this.

Also recognizing the interdependence of the church as well as its independence, the pastor will assume denominational and ecumenical responsibilities as energy, time, and opportunity afford.

In the pursuit of these duties, both pastor and congregation will recognize that there is a natural tension between being a leader of God's people and being an efficient administrator of ecclesiastical machinery. Easy solutions will not be found, but through single-minded orientation of all to the cause and person of Jesus Christ, the will of God surely can be found and done.

Chapter 16

Details of Administration

There are several details of church administration that are often taken for granted and thus overlooked. Churches are composed of human beings, which is another way of saying that churches are subject to the faults, errors, and problems which confront other institutions. Being a church does not absolve the organization from situations arising from these limitations.

A VOLUNTARY ORGANIZATION

The church, it must be emphasized, is a voluntary organization. In a culture which features separation of church and state and which offers wide latitude in the expression of individual liberty, it would seem that this principle would be understood very well.

135

It may be understood, but the companion doctrine of personal responsibility is often observed in the breach.

Two factors of administration must be stressed at this point. In the first place, church officers who furnish poor performance in the pursuit of their duties can be dismissed only with difficulty. Usually there is no constitutional authority by which this may be accomplished, and even more commonly there is the reluctance to "hurt feelings." Seldom can inefficient officers be eased out of position without rending the fabric of the church. Leaders and members of the congregation who are administrators of institutions employing large numbers of workers and who, perforce, must maintain discipline and dedication to the work at hand, often do not understand the problem of the church at this point.

On the other hand, members and officers are sometimes inclined to behave as though they were giving the church second place in their lives. Since there is no time clock, no supervisor of employment, and no production standards, members become sloppy in the performance of their responsibilities. Can anything be done? Certainly. They can be asked to resign! At the very least the church constitution can provide for limited terms and rotation in office.

MEETINGS

People often will say of church meetings, "We don't want to meet just to be meeting." And from this logical objection to gathering without purpose, regular committee meetings will be abandoned for the seemingly more logical position of getting together when need arises. Unfortunately, what usually arises from such procedure is that much business will be neglected, little creative action will be devised, and not much will be accomplished. It is difficult to imagine a church committee that doesn't have some business to transact. If it really has none, then it ought to examine how well it is fulfilling its responsibility. Therefore, it is strongly recommended that a committee meet monthly or at a minimum of nine times a year. These sessions will be for the assignment of tasks, the report of efforts attempted, the planning of special programs, and general administration.

PERSONNEL

All committee members and workers should be nominated by the chairperson of that committee in consultation with the pastor and approved by the church diaconate or executive board. The volunteer or the self-appointed person is apt to be difficult to fit into the total administrative picture. Terms of responsibilities will usually be for one year. In most areas, the matters of public school schedule and vacation time for workers indicate that the church activity year ought to run from June to June. If this is the case, the opportunity is thus offered to the chairperson to have the summer months to thank the retiring committee members, ascertain the readiness of any to serve another term, and select new members to fill the roster. In some circumstances, June to August is a very active time in the community. In such cases, the interim period should come some other time in the year. At best, the appointment of new committee members and the planning of new programs should not coincide with the annual meeting of the congregation and the election of officers. New officers need to fill their positions for a while in order to be able to make wise judgments regarding personnel and program. By taking office, for instance, in January when many churches hold their elections and by working with an already established committee for six months, i.e., until June, the new chairperson is much better equipped to take affirmative action.

REPORTS

Reports should be made periodically to the advisory board or diaconate (whatever name is chosen for the executive committee of the church) and yearly to the congregation. It has been said, derogatorily, that of the making of reports there is no end. But reporting should not be disparaged. Committees and officers have been known to have engaged in activity so as not to be embarrassed with the awful phrase, "Sorry, no report." It may be granted that to follow that way is to pursue a low road, indeed, but following a low road is better than following no road.

Reports give direction and stimulation not only to the group or person making them but also to the larger receiving body. Furthermore, others can then see how the whole program of the church fits together and thus make better judgments accordingly.

All reports should be written. Much time is wasted in church board and business meetings by those who come without the discipline of having set down on paper their thoughts, aims, achievements, and requests. This kind of wandering oratory is a simple type of thievery. Time is precious. Multiplied by the number of persons present, the total amount in time can be staggering. Being late for roll call is also a kind of robbery. Action is delayed until a quorum is present; time is lost. Or progress ceases while the moderator brings the tardy ones up to date on matters before the board. Emergencies are understandable, but chronic lateness is inexcusable.

DECORUM

One ought not to have to say anything about good manners among Christians. Unfortunately, it is necessary. The board or committee should function as a committee of the whole in the transaction of business. This means that the simplest type of parliamentary procedure is to be followed. A chairperson will preside as moderator but will be free to engage in discussion (a matter not acceptable in conducting a congregational meeting). A clerk will take minutes, but these need not be done with the attention to detail which is required in an assembly of the church.

At all times, respect for one another should be shown. Differences of opinion are to be expected; indeed, they are to be sought. Few problems offer easy solutions. It is the arriving at an intelligent choice that is the challenge. No one should speak more than once until all have spoken. No one should be allowed to dominate the discussion. The chairperson is expected to conduct the committee sessions firmly. Any expression of personal animosity or attack upon another member should be stifled promptly. A member who is so lacking in the spirit of Christ will be no help to the church. Previous generations may have been too ready to dismiss members from the fellowship for conduct unbecoming to a Christian, but the twentieth-century churches have been too lax. Self-discipline is the best. If this does not suffice, the chair should rule. And if this does not occur, the church should be apprised of the matter and should act to reestablish good order. This may require a call upon the disturbing member by the pastor and one other person. It may require even "disfellowship," but what is needed should be done— and promptly. Festering wounds do not heal themselves. A pastor in the prime of life and in normal health was driven to suicide by some obstreperous board members. Another in like situation and condition experienced a desperately crippling heart attack before the church took action and dismissed the disturbing member. Both churches should have moved long before they did. Unchristian conduct, even bad manners, are inexcusable in the life of the church.

PLANNING

The annual planning conference is crucially important in the organizational life of the church. It should be held toward the close of the activity year for adequate evaluation and well enough in advance of the beginning of another year so that plans and programs may be supplied with personnel and equipment and integrated into an articulate whole. If the true activity year for the congregation begins in September, as it does for many, then the planning session could be held in May or June, and the total program could be adopted by the congregation at a quarterly business meeting in July and inaugurated in September. This schedule allows for input by the various members, approval by the church (Shouldn't a church have the opportunity to review what it is to be doing the next year?), the selection of committee members by the chairpersons involved, and the mimeographing or otherwise duplicating for general use copies of the program to be followed for the year. Such a program should include, also, a list of sermon topics and Scripture texts which the pastor plans to follow in the preaching schedule for the ensuing year. This information can be helpful to the music director in the selection of appropriate anthems, and the congregation may be encouraged to do some extra reading on the themes and biblical backgrounds. Stimulation for the pastor to prepare his or her messages and to avoid the Saturday night "emergency" sessions in the study is obvious. Last-minute planning usually results in last-place finishes.

Present at the planning session should be every officer and committee person in the church. In addition, all members should be welcome. At the minimum, the agenda should provide for a time of worship, an overview of the task at hand by the pastor, and an extended period for committee discussions as committees meet separately to evaluate last year's program and to outline in detail their particular goals and tasks for the year ahead. Of special importance is the setting of dates for various activities. Finally, there should be a plenary session when each committee presents its program for the coming year, with dates and details. After the close of the planning conference, and in the weeks immediately following, the pastor and the officers will adjust schedule conflicts and be prepared at a subsequent meeting of the congregation as a whole to present for adoption the church activity calendar for the year to come. A ship which is put in order before it sails, which has an adequate crew and a known port ahead has a reasonable chance of making it across the water. Unless these preparations are followed, who knows when, where, or even if a harbor will be reached. So it is with the local church. Drifting is not a part of the Great Commission.

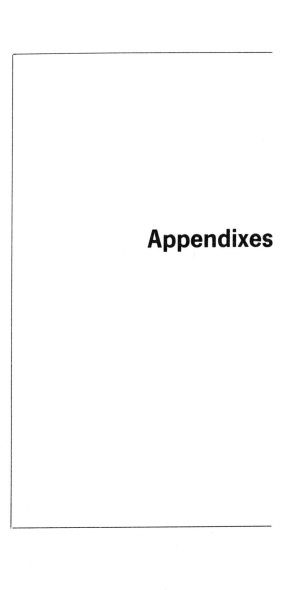

Appendixes

HOW ONE CHURCH CHANGED TO A SINGLE BOARD

In spite of years of harmonious relationship, the pastor and people of a midwestern church had become aware that something was amiss in their organizational life. So often they found themselves majoring on minor matters. Time and talent were being spent on nonessentials. Simply keeping the machinery of organization functioning was demanding too much of both administration and membership. As a result, the church decided upon a five-year plan to discover, form, and validate some new organizational procedures which might more effectively allow the ministry of Christ to be performed. The following is a summary of the major steps taken.

Year One: The congregation elected a "Church and Community Study Committee" to review the life and work of their total ministry. This survey revealed some frustrations with the current structure and found that there was "a general desire for a more effective, flexible, responsive, and responsible way of doing the church's work."

Year Two: The report of the "Church and Community Study Committee" was received with approval by the congregation and resulted in the appointment of a

"Study Committee on Organizational Procedure (SCOOP)." Five members, plus the pastor, were to form SCOOP and were charged with examining the current organizational structure, exploring alternatives, and recommending changes. Meetings of the committee were held, interviews with denominational leaders were conducted, and tentative ideas were presented to the congregation for review. Early in the process, it became clear that a statement on purpose for the congregation was needed for direction. This was prepared by the committee, reviewed and affirmed by the congregation, and established as the basis for developing structural changes.

Year Three: Proceeding from the foundation of purpose (form follows function), the committee (SCOOP) began to devise points for remodeling the organization. After a broad plan was developed, it was presented to a combined meeting of the various boards together with the several adult classes of the church. Comments and criticisms were heard and weighed. Some substantial changes in the presented form were later reviewed and adopted. A revised proposal was then introduced in a series of hearings with further modifications being included. The final form of a new organizational structure for the church was offered to the congregation and was adopted for a trial period of two years.

Year Four: The initial trial period for the new plan

included the suspension for two years of affected articles in the constitution. Substitute recommendations, or guidelines incorporating the new features, were adopted.

Year Five: The second year of the trial period culminated in a review of the new plan of organization and the revision of the new constitution in order to provide for the permanent reception of the project. In case the congregation had found the new scheme unwise or unworkable, the matter automatically would have become a dead issue and the organization would have reverted to the previous structure.

(Thanks to the First Baptist Church, Midland, Michigan, and its pastor, Dr. Joseph I. Mortensen, for these suggestions.)

APPENDIX B

MUSIC LEADERSHIP GUIDELINES

The following items are some detailed guidelines which one church developed to clarify some of the duties and responsibilities of its music staff. These staff people will normally be responsible to the Worship Committee.

THE ORGANIST

1. The Church Organist shall be responsible for playing the organ at the regular weekly church services and shall participate in the regular weekly rehearsals of the church choir.

2. When not able to attend Sunday services and/or choir rehearsals, the Church Organist shall be responsible for notifying the Worship Chairperson or the pastor of her or his inability to attend in order that an adequate substitute may be secured. Said notice shall be given at the earliest opportunity.

3. The Church Organist shall be responsible for a reasonable amount of special music at special services, or other occasions, when requested by the pastor or the Worship Chairperson. In the event the number of requests exceeds twelve per year, the Church Organist shall be compensated at the rate of twenty dollars per occasion in excess of that number.

4. The Church Organist shall be entitled to a total of four absences from Sunday services and/or choir rehearsals for sickness in any year without deduction from salary. Thereafter, deduction shall be made on a pro rata basis. In addition, she or he shall be entitled to a paid two weeks' vacation, same to include absence from both the Sunday service and the choir rehearsal during each week.

5. The Church Organist will be expected to practice weekly on the church organ, putting in the time necessary for him or her to become familiar with the music selected for the Sunday service and other musical services during the year.

6. If the person taking the position of Church Organist is not familiar with the particular organ being used by the church, that person should be willing to take a series of lessons on same.

7. The Church Organist shall be hired on a twelve-month basis, calendar year.

8. It shall be the responsibility of the Music Committee to see that the above guidelines are carried out to the satisfaction of all parties involved and for the enrichment of the music program of the church.

THE CHOIR DIRECTOR

1. The Choir Director shall be responsible for selecting, prior to the commencement of the church year beginning September 1, anthems and/or special

music to be performed by the choir during the church year. Prior to selecting a specific anthem for a particular Sunday, the Choir Director shall consult with the pastor in an effort to select an anthem that will be appropriate to the general theme of the sermon for that Sunday.

2. The Choir Director shall be responsible for the scheduling and directing of choir rehearsals.

3. The Choir Director in consultation with the choir members shall be responsible for scheduling the special music during the summer months.

4. When not able to attend Sunday services and/or choir rehearsals, the Choir Director shall be responsible for notifying the Worship Committee or the pastor, in that order, of his or her inability to attend in order that an adequate substitute may be secured. Said notice shall be given at the earliest possible opportunity.

5. The Choir Director shall be responsible for a reasonable amount of special music to be performed by the choir at special services, or on other occasions, when requested by the pastor or the Worship Chairperson. In the event the number of requests exceeds ten per church year, the Choir Director shall be compensated at the rate of twenty dollars per occasion in excess of that number.

6. The Choir Director shall be entitled to a total of four absences from Sunday services and/or choir rehearsals for sickness in any church year without deduction from salary. Thereafter, deduction shall be

made on a pro rata basis.

7. The Choir Director will be expected to spend time each week in studying the music to be used at choir rehearsals and Sunday services.

8. The Choir Director shall be hired on a ten-month basis, beginning on September 1 of each calendar year.

9. It shall be the responsibility of the Music Committee to see that the above guidelines are carried out to the satisfaction of all parties involved and for the enrichment of the music program of the church.

APPENDIX C

Sample Report Form for the Treasurer

DISBURSEMENTS	Current Year				Previous Year	
	Budget for year	Budget to date	Actual to date	Difference—Budget/Actual	Budget to date	Actual to date
Worship Service*						
Church Staff*						
Salaries	___	___		___	___	___
Benefits	___	___		___	___	___
Church Home*						
Utilities					___	___
Maintenance					___	___
Debt Retirement					___	___
Administration*					___	___
Missions*					___	___
TOTALS					___	___

*Show specific items as they are listed in the church budget for the year.

	Current Year				Previous Year	
INCOME	Budget for year	Budget to date	Actual to date	Difference—Budget/Actual	Budget to date	Actual to date
Pledges						
Plate						
Sunday School						
Missions						
Miscellaneous						
Designated*						
TOTAL	___	___	___	___	___	___
DISBURSEMENTS (carried from previous page)	___	___	___	___	___	___
SURPLUS (Income less disbursements)	___	___	___	___	___	___

*Designated Gifts detailed below.

APPENDIX D

CONSTITUTION

COMMUNITY BAPTIST CHURCH
Somerset, New Jersey

ARTICLE I. NAME

The name of this church shall be Community Baptist Church of Somerset.

ARTICLE II. PURPOSE

The purpose of this church shall be to persuade and assist people to adopt a new way of living under the control and possession of God; and, with Jesus Christ as head and the Bible as authority, to become an example of this Way. It shall seek to attain this end through the public worship of God, the preaching of the Gospel, missionary endeavor and Christian education.

ARTICLE III. MEMBERSHIP

Section A. Scope. Membership in this church shall be open to everyone who desires to be under the control and possession of God, who accepts Jesus Christ as Lord and Savior, and the Bible as authority, and who agrees to work under the provisions of this Constitution.

Section B. Procedure. The Council shall examine all

candidates for membership taking into consideration the recommendation of the Pastor. If approved by the Council, a candidate shall be voted upon by the congregation and if approved by a majority vote shall be received into the membership of the church with appropriate ceremony upon being baptized; or, if already a member of a Christian Church, upon presentation of evidence of his personal acceptance of Christ to the Council, such as a letter or statement.

Section C. Baptism. Baptism in this church will be only of believers and by immersion.

Section D. Associate Members. Students or other persons temporarily residing in the area and who are members in good standing of some other Christian Church may be received as associate members, following the same procedure and having all the privileges of regular members, without loss of membership in their home church; except that associate members shall not vote on amendments to this Constitution. Associate members shall not be counted in the public statistics of the church and shall be automatically dropped from the church roll upon leaving the area.

Section E. Termination of Membership. Termination of membership shall be

1. *By death.*
2. *By resignation.* A member's name shall be removed from the church roll upon receipt of a

written resignation and majority vote of the congregation. Verbal resignation shall not be recognized.

3. *By letter.* A member in good standing wishing to unite with another church may be given a letter of dismissal and recommendation by the Council certifying as to his standing in this church and commending him for church membership upon majority vote of the congregation.

4. *By suspension.* Any members, resident or non-resident, who fail to attend, give or serve through this church for a period of two years or more shall be placed on an inactive list for two additional years. During this time the church shall seek to do what it can to reactivate them. If at the end of this four year period they are still inactive, they shall be dropped from membership upon majority vote of the congregation. Notification of both their being placed on an inactive list and of their being dropped shall be sent to their last known residence.

5. *By Exclusion.* Any member whose conduct is flagrantly prejudicial to the good of the church, provided the Council feels action is necessary, shall, in accord with Matthew 18:15-20, be invited to appear before the Council to offer his defense. Mindful that the purpose of this section is reconciliation, every effort shall be made to resolve

the matter at this time. If it is not resolved he may be dropped from membership only by a two-thirds vote of the members present, qualified and voting at any business meeting of the church provided he has been given reasonable notice of said meeting and advised of his right to appear and present his defense.

ARTICLE IV. THE COUNCIL

Section A. Policy. The Council shall be the executive body of the church, having such powers as set forth in this Constitution and the by-laws of the church, including the powers normally exercised by Boards of Deacons, Deaconesses and Christian Education and legally exercisable by Trustees under N.J.S.A. 15: 1-1 et seq. In the exercise of these powers the Council may appoint such committees as it feels are necessary other than those committees expressly provided for elsewhere in this Constitution. The Council shall be responsible for the preparation of the church budget. The Council shall report at all regularly scheduled business meetings of the church and at special meetings if requested to do so.

Section B. Number and Term. The Council shall consist of twelve persons: the Moderator, Chairman of Christian Education, Clerk and Treasurer, each elected for a term of two years and eligible to serve two consecutive terms; and eight additional Councilmen (four of whom will be elected each year) elected to the positions specified under Section C, paragraphs 5 through 12, for a term of two years and eligible to serve two consecutive terms. Any person who shall have served two consecutive terms in any position or combination of positions on the Council shall be ineligible for reelection to any position on the Council until after spending one year out of office.

Section C. Duties of Council members. (Code in parenthesis indicates term of office and number of terms allowed.)

Paragraph 1. Moderator. (2 yr. x 2) The Moderator shall preside at all business meetings of the church and at all meetings of the Council, and have such other responsibilities as may be assigned in the Guidelines. He shall also have such powers as may be exercised by a president of a board of trustees under N.J.S.A. 15:1-1 et seq.

Paragraph 2. Clerk. (2 yr. x 2) The Clerk shall keep an accurate record of the action taken at all business meetings of the church and of the Council, see that permanent records of the church are preserved, and have such other responsibilities as may be assigned in the Guidelines.

Paragraph 3. Treasurer. (2 yr. x 2) The Treasurer, under the direction of the Council, shall be custodian of all church funds and securities. He shall keep, maintain, and preserve an accurate record of all receipts and disbursements. He shall be ready at any time, upon reasonable notice, to furnish the Council with information concerning the financial condition of the church. His records shall be audited annually by the Council and a full financial statement be presented to the church. He shall also have such other responsibilities as may be assigned in the Guidelines.

Paragraph 4. Chairman of Christian Education. (2 yr. x 2) The Chairman of Christian Education shall be charged with the total Christian Education program of the church, and have such other responsibilities as may be assigned in the Guidelines.

Paragraph 5. Evangelism Chairman. (2 yr. x 2) The Evangelism Chairman shall be charged with the responsibility of the church's outreach into the Community for the purpose of winning people to Jesus Christ and for membership in the church. He shall also have such other responsibilities as may be assigned in the Guidelines.

Paragraph 6. Hospitality Chairman. (2 yr. x 2) The Hospitality Chairman shall be charged with the cultivation of prospective members, and with such other responsibilities as may be assigned in the Guidelines.

Paragraph 7. Fellowship Chairman. (2 yr. x 2) The Fellowship Chairman shall be charged with the maintenance of the membership, and with such other responsibilities as may be assigned in the Guidelines.

Paragraph 8. Worship Chairman. (2 yr. x 2) The Worship Chairman shall be charged with the promotion and maintenance of a worshipful atmosphere for the public worship services of the church, and with such other responsibilities as may be assigned in the Guidelines.

Paragraph 9. Missions Chairman. (2 yr. x 2) The Missions Chairman shall be charged with keeping the church informed of the need and the work of our American Baptist World Mission and with such other responsibilities as may be assigned in the Guidelines.

Paragraph 10. Stewardship Chairman. (2 yr. x 2) The Stewardship Chairman shall be charged with the promotion and maintenance of Christian stewardship among the people of the church, and with such other responsibilities as may be assigned in the Guidelines.

Paragraph 11. Financial Secretary. (2 yr. x 2) The Financial Secretary shall be charged with the counting and recording of all contributions, and with such other responsibilities as may be assigned in the Guidelines.

Paragraph 12. Property Chairman. (2 yr. x 2) The Property Chairman shall be charged with the maintenance and improvement of all church property, and with such other responsibilities as may be assigned in the Guidelines.

ARTICLE V. NOMINATING COMMITTEE

The Nominating Committee shall consist of six members, three of whom shall be elected each year for a term of two years. No more than two members of the Council shall be members of the Nominating Committee. Members of the Nominating Committee shall not be eligible to serve for more than one consecutive term. Prior to the annual meeting, the Nominating Committee shall prepare a list of nominees to fill the various offices for which elections are to be held. It shall interview each nominee proposed and ascertain his or her willingness to serve if elected. During the year if vacancies in office occur, it shall present suitable nominations for filing these vacancies.

ARTICLE VI. PULPIT COMMITTEE

When the church comes to be without a Pastor, the Council shall nominate a Pulpit Committee at any regular or special meeting of the church. The nominations shall be subject to alterations and additions by the congregation, and the final nominations shall be subject to approval by two-thirds of the membership present, qualified and voting. The Pulpit Committee shall consist of not more than eleven persons and shall be elected with concern given to the various interests of the church. No more than three members of the Council shall be on the Pulpit Committee.

The Pulpit Committee shall seek information and

counsel on procedure from the New Jersey Baptist Convention and available literature on the choosing of a pastor. It shall analyze the needs of the church in the light of its current and prospective situation and effectiveness. It shall proceed to review prospects, their records and recommendations, interview one or more of them and submit the name of one candidate at a time to the congregation for their action.

ARTICLE VII. AFFILIATIONS

The church shall maintain affiliations with the Watchung Cluster, The American Baptist Churches in New Jersey, The American Baptist Churches of the U.S.A., the local Council of Churches, the New Jersey Council of Churches, the National Council of Churches and the World Council of Churches.

ARTICLE VIII. MEETINGS

Section A. Services. Public services shall be held on each Lord's Day.

The Lord's Supper shall be celebrated on the first Sunday of each month or on such other day as shall be determined upon by the Pastor and the Council, but in no event less than one time each month.

Occasional religious meetings may be scheduled by the Pastor, by the Council, or by a majority vote of the Church.

Section B. Business Meetings. The annual business meeting shall be held on or before the third Sunday in January for the purpose of receiving annual reports of the Council, individual officers, and committees of the church, and its auxiliary organizations, elections, and the transaction of such other business as is proper to come before the meeting.

Quarterly business meetings shall be held during the months of April, July and October of each year on a day to be determined by the Pastor and the Council. Notices of the dates of such meetings shall be given at least two weeks in advance of the dates of the same by publishing such notices in the church bulletin or announcing dates from the pulpit.

A quorum for the transaction of business shall consist of 15 members in good standing, of legal age.

Special meetings may be called at any time by the Pastor, the Moderator, or, upon the receipt of a petition of 5 members (no more than one being from any one family) of the church, by the Clerk. Notice of such meeting and the object for which it is called, shall be given at least one week in advance of the date of the meeting. At any of the regular meetings of worship, however, the church may, without notice, act upon the appointment of delegates to meetings, associations and conventions and may vote on candidates for membership and on termination of membership.

ARTICLE IX. THE PASTOR

A candidate for the pastorate shall be a member of a Baptist Church. Before his installation as Pastor, he shall become a member of this church, and if not already ordained shall be ordained. His election shall require the affirmative vote of two-thirds of the membership present, qualified and voting. He shall be an ex-officio member of all boards and committees but shall not serve as chairman of any board or committee.

ARTICLE X. ELECTIONS

Section A. Time. Annual elections shall be held during the annual meeting of the church.

Section B. Qualifications of Voters. All matters pertaining to the purchase, sale, or mortgaging of property shall be voted on only by members of legal age. On all other matters, all members are entitled to vote except as provided in ARTICLE III, Section D.

Section C. Procedure. At any election it shall be the privilege of any member present to place in nomination the name of any eligible person for any office. A majority of the ballots cast are necessary for election to any office.

Section D. Vacancies. Vacancies occurring during the year may be filled for the unexpired term at any business meeting. The Nominating Committee shall present to the church nominees for the vacancy to be filled. If more than one-half of the term of office for which the vacancy has occurred has expired on the date of the election to fill the vacancy, the person elected shall be eligible to serve as many additional full terms as are permitted under ARTICLE IV of this Constitution.

ARTICLE XI. STEWARDSHIP

Needs of the church and all of its departments should be financed through stewardship. The Church Council, however, may upon petition, approve activities it considers in keeping with the church's religious principles.

ARTICLE XII. PARLIAMENTARY AUTHORITY

The rules contained in Roberts' *Rules of Order Revised* shall govern meetings of the church in all cases to which they are applicable and in which they are not inconsistent with this Constitution.

ARTICLE XIII. CHURCH YEAR

The fiscal year of the church shall be the calendar year.

ARTICLE XIV. AMENDMENTS

Amendments to this Constitution may be made at any regular or special meeting of the church by a two-thirds vote of those present, qualified and voting, provided that any proposed amendment shall have been presented in writing at a business meeting of the church and distributed to all members at least four weeks before action is taken by the church.

NOTE: Appended to this Constitution as it is used by Somerset Church are Guidelines drawn up by the church to aid its officers in defining their roles and fulfilling their responsibilities. These guidelines embody the material found in chapters 6 through 14 of this book, as it has been specifically designed and adapted for use in the Somerset Church. The Preamble to the Guidelines states the following general principles:

 • The congregation has final authority in all matters.

 • The council is the legislative body and as such has responsibility for giving direction and insuring that the minister carries out the day-to-day functions.

 • The minister is the executive officer and as such is responsible to the council in carrying out the day-to-day functions under the supervision of the council.

 • The various officers and committee chairmen are responsible for carrying out the responsibilities in the guidelines under the general supervision of the minister.

Books
on Church
Administration

The following books contain helpful information on the various aspects of church administration. (All are published by Judson Press, Valley Forge, Pennsylvania.)

Asquith, Glenn H., *Church Officers at Work*, rev. ed., 1977.

Blazier, Kenneth D., *Building an Effective Church School*, 1976.

Blazier, Kenneth D., and Huber, Evelyn M., *Planning Christian Education in Your Church*, 1974.

Ellis, Loudell O., *Church Treasurer's Handbook*, 1978.

Grenell, Zelotes, and Goss, Agnes Grenell, *The Work of the Clerk*, 1967.

Huber, Evelyn M., *Enlist, Train, Support Church Leaders*, 1975.

Johnson, Alvin D., *The Work of the Usher,* 1966.

Madsen, Paul O., *The Person Who Chairs the Meeting,* 1973.

Maring, Norman H., and Hudson, Winthrop S., *A Baptist Manual of Polity and Practice,* 1963.

———, *A Short Baptist Manual of Polity and Practice,* 1965.

Massey, Floyd, Jr., and McKinney, Samuel Berry, *Church Administration in the Black Perspective,* 1976.

Merrill, R. Dale, *The Church Business Meeting,* 1968.

Nichols, Harold, *The Work of the Deacon and Deaconess,* 1964.

Rusbuldt, Richard E.; Gladden, Richard K.; and Green, Norman M., Jr., *Local Church Planning Manual,* 1977.

Thomas, Donald F., *The Deacon in a Changing Church,* 1969.

Tibbets, Orlando L., *The Work of the Church Trustee,* 1979.